My
Lyrical
Meanderings

Kevin M. Pitzer

"addressing one another in psalms and hymns and spiritual songs, singing and making melody to the Lord with your heart" (Ephesians 5:19).

Written Word Publishing LLC
14189 E Dickinson Drive, Unit F
Aurora, Colorado 80014
www.writtenwordspublishing.com

Published by Written Word Publishing LLC May 31, 2023

ISBN: 979-8-9873088-5-1 (paperback)
ISBN: 979-8-9873088-6-8 (eBook)

Library of Congress Control Number: 2023907798

Cover design by Bretech Solutions Group
www.bretechsolutions.com

Thank You, Father

Thank You, Father, for the care You have for
  me.
    Thank You, Father, for setting me free
From evil, from sin and for letting me in
    To Your loving, heavenly family
I love You. Amen.

Dedication

I am dedicating this book to my lovely wife, Nancy K. Pitzer, who has stood by me, supported me and loved me for decades. I cannot imagine life without you!

"He who finds a wife finds a good thing and obtains favor from the Lord" (Proverbs 18:22).

Contents

I am a Christian

I am a Christian, prepared to live my life, and give my life for the furtherance of God's Holy Kingdom. And He said to them, *"Go into all the world and proclaim the gospel to the whole creation"* (Mark 16:15).

I am simply a sinner, who does not deserve anything but eternal punishment in the torments of hell. But Jesus Christ took my sins upon Himself and died a horrible death on the cross for me. I asked Jesus into my heart, and He now is a vital part of my life, and I will dwell with Him forever. *"For God so loved the world, that he gave his only Son, that whoever believes in him should not perish but have eternal life"* (John 3:16).

I will never surrender my faith, my convictions, and my morals to societal pressures. I will remain true to my Lord and Savior, Jesus Christ. *"Therefore, my brothers, whom I love and long for, my joy and crown, stand firm thus in the Lord, my beloved"* (Philippians 4:1).

I will love sinners because I am also a sinner. I will try to live my life to show others that there is hope in Jesus. *"for all have sinned and fall short of the glory of God"* (Romans 3:23).

I will not judge others. I will not disparage others because of their sins, their beliefs and their sexual preference. I will try to be an example of God's Love to all of those I meet. I will let them

1

know that God's Faithful Love can and will overcome every sin. *"Judge not, and you will not be judged; condemn not, and you will not be condemned; forgive, and you will be forgiven;"* (Luke 6:37).

Society is our battleground and the world is at war with Satan and his demons. Though Satan will tempt me, I will resist. Though Satan tries to drag me down into sin, I will remain upright in God's Power. Though Satan tries to discredit me, I will continue to live my life for my Savior, Jesus Christ. *"...If God is for us, who can be against us?"* (Romans 8:31).

I will be willing to share my faith with whoever I meet. I will freely answer any question they have, using God's Holy Word as the basis for my answers. I will continue to follow the leading of the Lord and do what He wants me to. *"Behold, I stand at the door and knock. If anyone hears my voice and opens the door, I will come in to him and eat with him, and he with me"* (Revelation 3:20).

I will never forsake my fellowship with other believers, no matter who they are. This is important so we may encourage, comfort, and pray for each other. *"not neglecting to meet together, as is the habit of some, but encouraging one another, and all the more as you see the Day drawing near"* (Hebrews 10:25).

I will always remember that I am a Beloved Child of God. I will strive to live my life by His

Word. I will be dedicated to the Holy Bible, and to my Lord and Savior who has set me free from sin and the torments of hell. I will always trust in the Lord and in His teachings. *"Trust in the Lord with all your heart, and do not lean on your own understanding. In all your ways acknowledge him, and he will make straight your paths"* (Proverbs 3:5-6).

As I looked out on the world as it is today and saw how rapidly it was declining into sin and chaos, I wanted to declare my faith through this writing. There is a code of conduct that every military member swears by, and this piece was modeled after that code.

As I began to write this article, it took on a life of its own. However, I am pleased with the way it turned out. All of God's children need to live by a code that is based on God, the Bible, and their faith. This is the only way we can live and share in our world.

Kevin M. Pitzer, July 2015

<u>Good Morning, Jesus</u>

Good morning, Jesus, it's good to talk to You
    Ba, ba, ba, bump
Good morning, Jesus, I'm asking You to do,
    Be with me through the day
In everything I do or say
    Ba, bump
Good morning, Jesus, it's good to talk to You

Good morning, Jesus, I thank You for my wife
    Ba, ba, ba, bump
She is a beauty, and has really blessed my life
    Please surround her with the love
That comes from me and Heaven above
    Ba, bump
Good morning, Jesus, I thank You for my wife

*"I give you thanks, O' Lord, with my whole
heart; before the gods I sing your praise; I bow
down toward your holy temple and give thanks
to your name for your steadfast love and your
faithfulness, for you have exalted above all
things your name and your word"*
(Psalm 138:1-2).

<u>I Thank You</u>

Father above, I thank You for Your love
    And constant watch-care over me
I am never alone, no matter where I roam
    Your guiding touch I always see

Thank You for Your love, Your grace
    And Your loving embrace
And the promise that You made to me
    That one day I will see Your face
And dwell in a heavenly place
    With You, for eternity.
I love You. Amen.

7 January 2018

*"And whatever you do, in word or deed, do
everything in the name of the Lord Jesus, giving
thanks to God the Father through Him"*
(Colossians 3:17).

<u>Do Not Despair</u>

All is not lost
    For Christ paid the cost
To pay the price for our sin
    He loves us and helps us
If we just ask Him to come in
    So do not despair
For He is always there
    And will take us to Heaven with Him!

29 December 2017

"But we have this treasure in jars of clay, to show that the surpassing power belongs to God and not to us. We are afflicted in every way, but not crushed; perplexed, but not driven in despair; persecuted, but not forsaken; struck down, but not destroyed; always carrying in the body the death of Jesus, so that the life of Jesus may also be manifested in our bodies"
(II Corinthians 4:7-10).

One Day

One day I close my eyes
    And tell this world goodbye
And like the eagle from its nest
    I'll soar into the sky
With angels flying by my side
    I know I'll come to land
On the often-promised blessed shore
    Of the precious Holy Land

"If then you have been raised with Christ, seek the things that are above, where Christ is, seated at the right hand of God. Set your minds on things that are above, not on things that are on earth. For you have died, and your life is hidden with Christ in God. When Christ who is your life appears, then you also will appear with him in glory" (Colossians 3:1-4).

Throne of Grace

Let us go before the Throne of Grace,
    And reach out to God in prayer
We know that He will hear us
    for He is always there.

God may not give us what we want
    But He will always fill our needs
And He will always be there with us
    For He is God indeed.

2015

*"Let us then with confidence draw near to the
throne of grace, that we may receive mercy and
find grace to help in time of need"*
(Hebrews 4:16).

One of the most powerful weapons a
Christian has against evil is prayer. We have a
mighty, powerful and loving God who wants to
help us. He created the universe and everything
in it. He made each individual and wants the best
for each of us. He knew us before we were even

born. How can we not go before Him and ask for grace and blessings?

Oscar's Canes

When they went into the service
    They stood young, and brave, and tall
Ready to protect our great country
    And willing to give their all
They served with pride and honor
    In conditions tough to bear
But they knew that their country needed them
    And they bravely did their duty there
But battle and age take their toll
    And their bodies ache with pain
And with thanks and praise we honor them
    By blessing them with a cane
Now they stand so proud and tall again
    It's the least that we could do
To honor and to bless our veterans
    For the battles they went through
We ask You, Heavenly Father
    For our veterans everywhere
Please bless their homes and families
    And may their bodies feel Your care.
Amen

24 July 2016

Amen, Wow, that's beautiful. That was part of last night's subject, I was writing about. See? That just summed up a page and a half of writing. Kevin, I don't want to scare you. Veterans keep telling me God would bless me. I believe it's you.

10

We have such a story to tell. Oh, sending you a photo of your cane up on the rack.

Oscar De Vere Morris

"Let brotherly love continue. Do not neglect to show hospitality to strangers, for thereby some have entertained angels unawares"
(Hebrews 13:1-2).

Several years ago, I heard of a gentleman who made it his mission to make 500 canes for disabled veterans and to ship the canes to them, all free of charge. I applied for a cane and got to know Oscar in the process. He is a Navy veteran himself and desired to help out other veterans in need.

I do not remember how I found his Facebook page, but I am so glad I did. He has reached his goal of making 500 canes and is still making more.

It has been a blessing for me to know Oscar de Vere Morris on several levels. First as a fellow veteran and next as the creator of my cane. Oscar is also a brother-in-Christ. I do appreciate his dedication, generosity and for using his God-given talents to enrich the lives of others.

Each cane he makes is made with the love Oscar has for God. Each cane is carefully crafted, personalized for the veteran, and prayed over before it is sent to the recipient. Oscar has been a blessing to many people on so many levels. He has had some setbacks, but he continues to work his ministry and trust God. Thank you, Oscar!

500 Canes (And Counting)

He started with a goal in mind
    To make 500 canes
To distribute free to veterans
    Who are crippled and in pain
It started small, then grew so large
    With veterans who were in need
He went into his shop and made man glitter
    And kept busy indeed
And with each cane he said a prayer
    To God the Father up above
That each cane would bless its veteran
    And to share with them God's love
Now Oscar's goal is finished
    The final canes packed and ready to go
He blessed the lives of 500 vets
    His love for God and country showed
From the veterans across this great land
    A giant Hooyah shouts out for him
The veterans all thank you, Brother Oscar
    For your faithfulness to them
You've changed the lives of 500 vets
    And helped them stand proud and tall
Your reward is waiting in Heaven
    Because you gave your all

3 October 2016

Thank you, Brother, love you!

"Through him then let us continually offer up a sacrifice of praise to God, that is, the fruit of lips that acknowledge his name. Do not neglect to do good and to share what you have, for such sacrifices are pleasing to God"
(Hebrews 13:15-16).

My Oscar Cane

For many months I waited
    In rapt anticipation
For a small reward that I'd receive
    For my service for our nation
But it was well worth the wait
    For the cane that I received
The cane that Oscar had made
    Perfectly captured my personality
My service in the Air Force
    Was prominently displayed
And my dedication to the Lord
    Is what the cane seems to say
I am so honored to receive this gift
    From a fellow Brother in the Lord
Making these canes may not pay much
    But great is Oscar's eternal reward
Hooyah!

Fill Our Pews

Oh, Father of the Harvest,
　　we bring this plea to You

Please bless our church with people
　　and fill our empty pews

Each pew has the potential
　　to show people of Your love

To build them up in Your Gospel
　　help us bring the world to You

Our church is not just a building,
　　but people of one mind

Who want to love You and to serve You
　　and share You all the time

Though we are small in numbers
　　we want to work for You

Father, hear our humble plea
　　and fill our empty pews

*"...Look, I tell you, lift up your eyes, and see
that the fields are white for harvest"*
(John 4:35).

16

We attend a small country church. It is sometimes discouraging to see how many seats are empty on Sunday mornings. Our pastor once preached a sermon about how we needed to grow and reach out into our community. His prayer at the end of the service was for God to fill our empty pews.

Since that sermon, our church has grown and is continuing to grow. We continue to pray and work for more people to fill our pews.

Bibles in Back Windows

I see Bibles in back windows
    Of cars that are passing by
It really gets me to thinking
    And I often wonder why

Are they used only on Sundays
    To look pious in church
Or are they quickly ruffled through
    When their owner's in a lurch?

Does your Bible sit on a table
    For everyone to see
Or is it a vital part of your life
    Praying, "God, please impact me"?

We really need the Bible
    And to read it every day
So we can receive God's guidance
    To lead us on His way

Be open to God's Word, my friend
    By staying in His Word
And you will be pleasantly surprised
    At your impact for the Lord

24 January 2016

"So put away all malice and all deceit and hypocrisy and envy and all slander. Like newborn infants, long for the pure spiritual milk, that by it you may grow up into salvation—if indeed you have tasted that the Lord is good" (I Peter 2:1-3).

Our pastor used to be a truck driver. He has a wonderful testimony of how the prayers and persistence of his parents brought him to the Lord. He related to us in a sermon that while driving his truck, he would notice how many people had Bibles laying by the back window in their cars. He also wondered if people took the Word seriously and were consistently in the Word of God.

I got inspired by this illustration and, "Bibles in Back Windows," was born.

<u>Through Life's Troubles</u>

Through all of life's troubles
 Disappointments, hurts and pains
One thing always keeps me going
 Knowing Christ will come again

As the world around us degenerates
 And embraces all types of sin
I need to be an example
 That in Christ we can win

He knows us all and loves us
 And wants to be our eternal friend
Just ask Him into your heart and life
 And you will never be alone again

I have my hope based on Jesus
 For great blessings and forgiveness of sins
And when I step into the Great by and by
 I will live forever with Him

Thank You, Father and Jesus the Son
 For being my eternal friend
And for giving me the Great hope in You
 I love You, Father, Amen

4 February 2019

*"but they who wait for the Lord shall renew
their strength; they shall mount up with wings
like eagles; they shall run and not be weary;
they shall walk and not faint"* (Isaiah 40:31).

We, as Christians living in a fallen world, are constantly beset by troubles. We constantly see how the world is deteriorating every day, yet it continues to reject Christ. Our personal lives are sometimes in shambles. Financial problems, relationship issues and illness plague us all, but God's children have hope in Christ and we need to be willing to share that hope with a world that desperately needs it.

I've Failed You, Lord

So many times, I've failed You, Lord
    I do it every day
My intentions are always good
    But I sometimes lose my way
I know I hurt You deeply, Lord
    It makes me feel so bad
But when I ask for Your forgiveness
    You accept it, and I'm glad

There was a time I had no hope
    Just a soul lost, wandering around
Then I met my blessed Savior
    And His love did astound
He gave me life eternal
    And a mansion up in Heaven
But most of all, He took my life
    And freed it from all sin!

Thank You, Thank You, Jesus
    For all You've done for me
For making me sin free in front of God
    By dying on the tree
I cannot wait to get to Heaven
    I want to hug and hug You again
You are my perfect Savior
    I love You, Lord. Amen.

October 2015

"for the righteous falls seven times and rises again, but the wicked stumble in times of calamity" (Proverbs 24:16).

So many times, in my life I have failed the Lord. I try to do things on my own, I do some that is against what He wants for me and my outright sin. It is discouraging when I realize this, but God always loves me and always wants what is best for me. I need to constantly remind myself how great our God is.

Helpless

Lord, at times I feel so helpless
    I don't know what to do
Have I offended You that much
    For what I'm going through

I try so hard to love You
    And to live life by Your Word
Why am I being punished
    It really hurts me Lord

But then I stop and realize
    That You are with me all the way
You always walk beside me
    Through every single day

I am sorry that I doubted You
    Please forgive me of my sin
Because when You are by my side
    I can do nothing but win

I love You, Lord, and thank You
    For the good times and the bad
You are faithful, Lord and loving
    The best thing that I have

October 2015

"I lift up my eyes to the hills. From where does my help come? My help comes from the Lord, who made heaven and earth" (Psalm 121:1-2).

My wife and I have been through so much over the last year or so. We have dealt with cancer, heart issues, surgeries, and a myriad of other problems that plague us. It seems like we are helpless and hopeless at times, but we always need to remember that God is much bigger than any of our problems.

Satan is Defeated

Our world is full of trouble
    Anger, hate and sin
We sit back and wonder
    Why Satan seems to win

But Satan is defeated
    His reign will soon be done
Because when Christ died on the Cross
    The battle had been won

Take heart my fellow Christians
    For the battle has been won
We have peace and eternal security
    Through Jesus Christ the Son

7 August 2016

"For I am sure that neither death nor life, nor angels nor rulers, nor things present nor things to come, nor powers, nor height nor depth, nor anything else in all creation, will be able to separate us from the love of God in Christ Jesus our Lord" (Romans 8:38-39).

When we take a look at our world, Christians can become mighty disappointed and feel hopeless. It seems like every day we see where Satan has won another victory. Crime, anger, hatred, and cruelty always seem to be taking over our society. Do not be discouraged, my friend! Keep up the good fight, trust in the Lord for all of His children will be victorious! Thank You, Jesus for the hope You give Your children.

<u>Instantaneously</u>

When a person sees the Love of God
    And accepts Christ into their heart
Instantaneously they become a Child of God
    And their life has a brand-new start

Their sins are all forgiven
    The Holy Spirit fills their soul
No longer can Satan run their life
    For God is in control

When I wake up in the morning
    Ready to start my day
Let me have Your praises on my mind
    To start me on my way

When I am driving down the highway
    Maybe heading off to work
Please put Your praises on my lips
    Rather than call someone a jerk

When I sit down at the table
    With my family by my side
Help me to thank You for all Your blessings
    And for You being by my side

When the day is finally over
    And I lay down in my bed
Help me to gently go to sleep
    With Your praises in my head

16 January 2016

When we ask the Lord to come into our hearts, we are instantly a part of His family. There are a whole lot of perks that go with this, but we will have to wade through the swamps of evil on this planet, showing God's love and forgiveness to everybody.

Our attitude will change, we will have the power to lose bad habits and we will be a recipient of the blessings of God. I have never regretted becoming a child of the Creator.

"May the God of hope fill you with all joy and peace in believing, so that by the power of the Holy Spirit you may abound in hope"
(Romans 15:13).

Every Second

Every second, every minute, every hour, every day
    I want to trust You, Jesus, in all I do or say
Every moment, let me thank You
    For Your constant, loving care

You will always stand beside me
    Anytime and anywhere
I know You will always love me
    Forgive me and always care

Every person that I see, Lord
    Help me spread the Word of You
How You can change a person's life
    And for all You see me through

I love You so much, Lord Jesus
    Thank You for being my friend
And I will stand by You and Your grace
    Until the very end.

18 November 2017

Although it is tough to do, we need to always
keep our minds on Christ and what He has done

and will do for us. Just think of what Christ has done for us on the Cross.

God has loved me so much, so completely and so unreservedly that I need to constantly pray to Him, thanking Him for what He has done for me. Every second of my life is a precious, God given blessing and are limited. I need to follow Him and to trust Him in every aspect of my life.

"Thanks be to God through Jesus Christ our Lord! So then, I myself serve the law of God with my mind, but with my flesh I serve the law of sin" (Romans 7:25).

Praise Him

We need to praise Him in the morning
    At the start of a new day
To thank Him for the opportunities
    To show others about His Way

We should praise Him in the noontime
    When things are going wrong
For He still loves and walks beside us
    With every step the whole day long

We should praise Him in the evening
    For all the times that He has seen us through
And the times He has led us, taught us,
  comforted us
    Through everything we say and do

Thank You, Father, for all that You have done
  for me
    For taking away all my sins, and from Satan
      set me free
Thank You, Heavenly Father for the good, the
  bad, the pain
    For I know that no matter what I go through
      on this earth
Some day, with You in Heaven I will reign

13 January 2017

"giving thanks always and for everything to God the Father in the name of our Lord Jesus Christ" (Ephesians 5:20).

My lovely wife and I have been through some tough times health-wise. We do not know why, but we know we are in the hands of the loving God.

Recently, I received word from the VA, that I am going to need a heart catheterization. I was thankful they found something during my stress test, but a little bit scared of the heart procedure, poor Nancy was in tears. We simply need to put it all into God's hands.

I have never been to a cardiologist before, let alone, getting the authorization from the VA for the procedure, but within a matter of hours, I had a cardiologist, authorization, and an appointment with him next week. Even the VA was impressed with how fast everything was accomplished! I told them that God was in control!

Father, please give my wife and I comfort, as we face yet another round of medical issues. We know we need to lean on You, but sometimes we want to carry the burden alone, which will only make things worse. Thank You for being there, for caring intensely for every one of Your children, and for promising us a future in Heaven with You. I love You. Amen.

<u>Dear Father, Above</u>

Dear Father, above
    Help me to show my love
By walking and talking with You
    Help me to be a good son
Share the battles You have won
    By trusting and leaning on You
Let the world truly see
    That You are living in me
And that it is something they need to do
    To trust in You Lord
To follow Your Word
    And to live a life dedicated to You
Thank You for loving me, Lord
    And for keeping Your Word
And thank You for being my friend
    Help me to walk by Your side
And to keep my heart open wide
    To praise You and You. Amen.

23 January 2018

*"And we know that for those who love God all
things work together for good, for those who are*

*called according to his purpose. For those
whom he foreknew he also predestined to be
conformed to the image of his Son, in order that
he might be the firstborn among many brothers"*
(Romans 8:28-29).

Thank You for Your Presence

We thank You for Your presence, Lord
    We thank You for Your love
We thank You for the guidance
    You send down from above

We praise You for Your love and care
    We pray that what you'll do
Is keep us just and true until
    We come back home to You.

I love You. Amen.

22 April 2018

One of the most awesome promises in the Scriptures is, *"I will never leave you nor forsake you"* (Hebrews 13:5). To me, this means that no matter what problems we face, what issues we go through or what good times we experience, God is right there beside us! How wonderful is it that God, our Savior and the Creator of the universe, is always by our side? It gives me chills just to think about it.

"Be strong and courageous. Do not fear or be in dread of them, for it is the Lord your God who goes with you. He will not leave you or forsake you" (Deuteronomy 31:6).

Lord, Thank You

Lord, thank You for the sunshine
    Thank You for the rain
Thank You for the promise
    That You will be back again

Thank You for my family
    My children and my wife
And for all of our grandchildren
    That all enrich our life

Thank You for the blessings
    You give to me each day
Even though I don't deserve them
    They all brighten my way

Thank You for the problems
    The difficulties and woe
For they help me to depend on You
    As on this Christian walk, I go

I thank You, Lord for loving me
    For Your amazing grace
Please keep me loving and thanking You
    Until I come to stay at Your place

22 November 2018

"Rejoice always, pray without ceasing, give thanks in all circumstances; for this is the will of God in Christ Jesus for you"
(I Thessalonians 5:16-18).

We need to always praise God in all of our circumstances. We need to praise and thank Him for the good times and for the bad times. The good times for the blessings and the bad times that teach us to rely and lean on Him more.

<u>There is Hope in You</u>

We are really getting desperate, Lord
    It makes me want to cry
Our country is going downhill
    They don't care why You died

But there is hope in You, Lord
    As long as Your children are here
Keep us strong and faithful, Lord
    As Your time draws near

Keep us strong and praying, Lord
    Help us to spread Your Love
We really need revival, Lord
    It can only come from above

We know the time is getting close
    Because Your Word is true
Help us to never forget, Lord
    That our hope is in You!

    The world that we live in seems to be hopeless. Every day we hear of wars, humans' inhumanity to other humans and a general lack of respect for anything or anyone. There is an epidemic of hatred in our country like I have never perceived in my life. Sexual immorality of all kinds is being praised and the wholesale murder of innocent babies is applauded by some.

Yet, we still have a hope in Jesus Christ our Lord. He gives us the hope for His peace, His grace and His promise of eternal life. We need to rely on Him and be lighthouses for Him in this dark world.

"For this light momentary affliction is preparing for us an eternal weight of glory beyond all comparison, as we look not to the things that are seen but to the things that are unseen. For the things that are seen are transient, but the things that are unseen are eternal" (II Corinthians 4:17-18).

Preach It

Preach it, preacher, preach it
    Don't be afraid to spread the Word
Because people need to hear it
    And to get right with the Word

Teach it, Christians, teach it
    We are called to share the Lord too
So, show His Love and Saving Grace
    In all you say or do

Live it, God's people, live it
    Keep your life on God's track
We have to work diligently
    For Christ will soon come back

One of the commandments that God's children are given in the Scriptures is to preach and share the Word of God. We are all His witnesses and need to spread His love to everyone we can.

"And Jesus came and said to them, 'All authority in heaven and on earth has been given to me. Go therefore and make disciples of all

nations, baptizing them in the name of the
Father and of the Son and of the Holy Spirit,
teaching them to observe all that I have
commanded you. And behold, I am with you
always, to the end of the age'"
(Matthew 28:18-20).

God's Church Unite

Unite together, God's Church on earth,
    Put aside your petty quarrels,
For only by working together for God,
    Can we impact the world!

We all believe in Jesus Christ,
    Who was born of a virgin,
That He died on the cross and conquered death
    To save us all from sin!

We all know Christ is coming back
    His trumpet blast will be loud
He will take us home, but we need to work
    To increase that ascending crowd!

Unite with fellow Christians,
    Encourage each other and pray,
If we work together, through the Love of Christ,
    We can change our world today!

2015

We live in a world that is angry, disrespectful, and confused. However, we Christians have the

45

answer to the world's problems, Jesus Christ. We need to be of one mind with other churches to show a united front, firmly based on the Scriptures.

We cannot let our religions, our traditions and our differences separate us. We need to get back to the doctrines that are based in the Bible. We need to get back to the basics to effectively preach the Word. We need to be one united army of the Lord to show the world the love of Christ.

"until we all attain to the unity of the faith and of the knowledge of the Son of God, to mature manhood, to the measure of the stature of the fullness of Christ, so that we may no longer be children, tossed to and fro by the waves and carried about by every wind of doctrine, by human cunning, by craftiness in deceitful schemes. Rather, speaking the truth in love, we are to grow up in every way into him who is the head, into Christ," (Ephesians 4:13-15).

Preach the Gospel

Preach the Gospel through your life
    Live your life by God's Word
For your actions and the way, you live
    Could bring someone to the Lord

Lean on the Lord throughout your life
    Ask Him what you should do
So, you can be a living Gospel
    'til your work on earth is through

Oh, Father, take and mold me
    And fill me with Your might
Because I want to be for You
    A little, living, breathing light

As children of God, we are commanded to share His Word wherever we are and whatever we are doing. Can you imagine the effect it would have on society if every Christian unashamedly shared the Gospel?

"preach the word; be ready in season and out of season; reprove, rebuke, and exhort, with complete patience and teaching"
(II Timothy 4:2).

47

Pray, Pray, Pray

Pray, pray, pray
    Each hour of the day
Ask God for His Guidance
    To lead you on your way
Put your prayer pants on
    Get on your knees
And here's what you can say...

"Thank You, Lord, for saving me,
    From death apart from You
Please help me to show your Love,
    In all I say or do"

"Please be with the sick and hurting,
    Help the doctors to cure their ills
Please bless them and be with them
    And keep them in Your Will"

"Put Your Hand upon our country, Lord
    And those who You put in charge
Make Yourself known to them,
    As loving, faithful and large"

"Bring our country to revival, Lord
    Make us get down on our knees
And to call upon our Jesus
    To help our country, please"

"Thank You for all You've done for me
    My family, church and friends
For my salvation and my health, Lord
    And Your love that never ends"

"I love You, Lord, I need You, Lord
    To protect and keep me from sin,
I can't wait to live with You
    In Jesus' Name, Amen"

One of the basic privileges we have as Christians is the freedom to come before the throne of God and bring our praises and petitions to Him. It can be a simple prayer, talking to Him as a friend. We need to realize the power we have at our disposal through prayer.

I am not perfect, and it is sometimes hard for me to pray, but God knows our hearts and understands our pleas. God loves us and wants to help us, but we need to come before Him in prayer.

"O my God, incline your ear and hear. Open your eyes and see our desolations, and the city that is called by your name. For we do not present our pleas before you because of our righteousness, but because of your great mercy" (Daniel 9:18).

I Praise You, Lord

Lord, though it is cold outside
    Our hearts are warm
Because You tell us
    You will keep us from harm.

As we gather together
    Help us to focus on You
And to thank You, Father
    For all that You do.

I praise You, Lord
    For being my friend,
And now, as forever,
    I love You. Amen.

15 October 2017

"For great is the Lord, and greatly to be praised; he is to be feared above all gods. For all the gods of the peoples are worthless idols, but the Lord made the heavens. Splendor and majesty are before him; strength and beauty are in his sanctuary" (Psalm 96:4-6).

God, Thank You

God, thank You for being with us
    Through sunshine and through rain
For loving, guiding, helping us
    Until You come again

Life in this world is not easy
    We seem to fight against the tide
But we are promised and assured
    You will be by our side

Please help us now, Heavenly Father
    As we try to stand for You
Give us wisdom, peace and comfort
    Through the battles we go through

Thank You, Heavenly Father
    For our family and friends
And all the love that surrounds us
    I love You, God. Amen.

1 February 2017

"give thanks in all circumstances; for this is the
will of God in Christ Jesus for you"
(I Thessalonians 5:18).

Thank You, Father

Thank You, Father, for the care You have for me
    Thank You, Father, for setting me free
From evil, from sin and for letting me in
    To Your loving, heavenly family

I love You. Amen.

6 April 2018

*"Praise the Lord! Oh give thanks to the Lord,
for he is good, for his steadfast love endures
forever! Who can utter the mighty deeds of the
Lord, or declare all his praise?"*
(Psalm 106:1-2).

When I Finally Get to Heaven

When I finally get to Heaven
    and walk on Glory's shore

I will see my friends and family
    like I never had before

We will have celestial bodies
    that know no tears or pain

When I finally get to Heaven
    and we see each other again

When I finally get to Heaven
    and reach the Pearly Gate

It will be a grand reunion
    Oh, I can hardly wait

I see all of my family
    and grandchildren who've gone before

When I finally get to Heaven
    and walk through that Pearly door

When I finally get to Heaven
    I will see my Lord face to face

I will fall at His feet and thank Him
    for all His love and grace

I will then stand up and hug Him
    for all He's done for me

When I finally get to Heaven
    My Savior, Jesus I will see

I love being here on earth
    my friends and family I enjoy

But life can be so hard sometimes
    and circumstances annoy

One day, Christ will call me
    and to Heaven I will rise

To attend that great reunion
    up in God's Heavenly skies.

I'm going to Heaven! I know because Jesus told me I was. It is so exciting to know that one day I will shed this decrepit body of mine and go to my Lord and Savior in a brand-new, perfect body that will never grow old! I will see my mom and dad, all my family and friends who made the choice to follow Christ. I can hardly wait to move into my new mansion in Heaven! Thank you, Jesus.

"But, as it is written, 'What no eye has seen, nor ear heard, nor the heart of man imagined, what God has prepared for those who love him'"
(I Corinthians 2:9).

I am excited!

A Tiny Hand

As we sat in Sunday's service
    With my grandson by my side
This four-year-old could not sit still
    No matter what we tried

But then the pastor said, "Let us pray"
    Then Joshua sat quiet and still
With his eyes closed and his head bowed
    As the pastor asked for God's will

Then I felt his small sweaty palm
    Slip softly into my hand
And he held Pa-pa's hand tightly
    Until the pastor said Amen

Train up a child in the way he should go
    And he will never stray
That verse and Joshua's hand touched my heart
    In the quiet church that day

When he grows a little older
    And troubles come his way
He will always know that Pa-pa is there
    To take his hand and pray

11 September 2016

This was a special Sunday for me. Our grandson, Joshua, was sitting beside me in church. He has been coming to church since he was born. He was four-years-old at the time and was a little bit rambunctious, as all small boys will be.

The pastor prepared to pray and asked everyone to bow their heads. To my surprise, Joshua bowed his head and placed his hand in mine as we prayed. I was immensely pleased and glad that Joshua prayed with me. It touched my heart and gave me confidence that he was being brought up in a Christian home.

"Hear, my son, your father's instruction, and forsake not your mother's teaching, for they are a graceful garland for your head and pendants for your neck" (Proverbs 1:8-9).

Joshua's Prayer

Before the start of classes
　　At the beginning of the day
A moment of silence was held by the students
　　And our young grandson kneeled down in
　　　prayer

A small boy, kneeling by his desk
　　With his hands clasped in prayer
Is a wonderful picture of child-like faith
　　And the courage that he showed there

We could all follow this young boy's example
　　And start our day with a chat with God
To reach out to Him and to thank Him
　　For His help as through the day we trod

So, let's follow Joshua's example
　　As we start out our busy day
There is always a chance to take the time
　　To reach out to God and to pray

28 September 2017

At this point, Joshua is in a public-school kindergarten. As his class starts their day of learning, they have a quiet time where the children can sit quietly and prepare for the day. This day, his teacher sent Joshua's mother a picture of Joshua, kneeled down in front of his desk, hands folded and praying.

We live in a world where people are ridiculed and chastised for their faith. It set a good example and took some courage for Joshua to pray in front of his peers. Yes, he is young, but this act gave his classmates an example to not be afraid to live out your faith. I expect some great things from this young man.

"...Let the children come to me; do not hinder them, for to such belongs the kingdom of God. Truly, I say to you, whoever does not receive the kingdom of God like a child shall not enter it"
(Mark 10:14-15).

Speak to Me, Father

Speak to me, Father
    Lead me forward through Your Word

Give me the grace and courage
    To always live for the Lord

I want to feel You daily
    To feel Your peace and love

I know that I cannot truly live
    Without Your help from above

I know I always need You, Lord
    In times of blessing and despair

The one thing I always count on
    Is that You are always there

You knit my bones and body together
    While in my mother's womb

You knew me from conception, Lord
    And are with me to my tomb

July 2018

In the book of I Samuel, God is calling to young Samuel while he is in bed. God called him twice, and on the third time, *"And the Lord came and stood, calling as at other times, 'Samuel! Samuel!' And Samuel said, 'Speak, for your servant hears'"* (I Samuel 3:10).

We, as the children of God, should always be prepared to hear God so He can work through our lives. We need to take a time every day when we can get alone with God and fellowship with Him. If you want to get to know somebody better, you spend time with them. The same goes for your relationship with God.

Make Me a Beacon

Please make me a beacon, Lord
    I want to live for You
Help me to show Your love
    In all I say and do
I want to be a vessel, Lord
    That spreads Your love to men
I thank You lots and praise You
    I love You, Lord. Amen.

It is frustrating for me to see how our world is devolving into chaos because of the hate that is prevalent in society. Every day, we hear of good people being brought down by people holding them to an impossible standard that the accusers don't even live by!

If one gets into the public eye, they are immediately inundated with accusations and incidents from their past. Everybody makes mistakes and the ever-present social media is the perfect platform to tear people apart.

No one is perfect. We all have secrets and issues that we would like to keep that way. We need to remember this when we accuse and defame people. The same thing could happen to us in a heartbeat. We could find ourselves being vilified just as quickly and aggressively.

We also need to remember the only way that we can have the peace, the joy, and the contentment we all desire is to turn to Jesus. He is our only hope, our only salvation, and the only forgiveness we need. We can make a positive difference in our world and the only way to effectively accomplish this is through and in Christ.

"You are the light of the world. A city set on a hill cannot be hidden. Nor do people light a lamp and put it under a basket, but on a stand, and it gives light to all in the house. In the same way, let your light shine before others, so that they may see your good works and give glory to your Father who is in heaven"
(Matthew 5:14-16).

Good Morning, Heavenly Father

Good morning, Heavenly Father
    I thank You for today
For the sunshine and the blessings
    That You send to me each day

I thank You for the problems
    The heartache and the pain
For it reminds me daily, Father
    To rest in your Holy Name

Every day I want to praise You
    For the sunshine and the rain
And for that ever looked to promise
    That You will come back again

Thank You for the strength You give me
    To love and care for fellow men
For the love and grace You give us
    I love You, Father. Amen.

16 May 2018

*"Praise the Lord! Oh give thanks to the Lord,
for he is good, for his steadfast love endures
forever! Who can utter the mighty deeds of the
Lord, or declare all his praise?"*
(Psalm 106:1-2).

<u>Good Morning, Lord</u>

Good morning, Lord, I am about
    To start another week
Help me to share You with those
    Who for comfort and hope and peace seek

I know that You will work through me
    To bring others to Your love

Help me to be the one to show
    Your forgiveness from above
And as I dwell in our enemy's camp
    Please keep me away from sin
Keep me strong and on Your path
    And to trust in You my friend

For when my journey is over
    And I finally reach the end
I know I will live in Glory forever
    I love You, Father. Amen.

19 March 2018

Jesus has blessed us so much that we should always be praising, glorifying and thanking Him.

What better way could there be than to start the day communing with the Creator. He loves us so much and wants to hear from us and is just waiting to bless us for our faithfulness. What an overwhelming Savior!

"O Lord, in the morning you hear my voice; in the morning I prepare a sacrifice for you and watch" (Psalm 5:3).

Bidding This World Goodbye

One day, I'll close my eyes
    And bid this world goodbye
I soar into the sky above
    With angels by my side
They will lead me up to Glory Land
    Right to the Pearly Gate
And there I will meet Jesus
    And see Him face-to-face

Praise the Lord, I will see Jesus
    Praise the Lord my journey's done
My life for Him is completed
    And I am finally home

I will see my friends and family there
    And grandchildren who've gone before
I'll meet the saints from olden times
    And oh, there will be much more
I'll walk on streets of gold
    And see the glorious shore
Live in a mansion of my own
    With saints who live next door

I will keep on working for Him
    As I live my life below
I will show Jesus through my life
    To folks wherever I go
To bring others to our Savior
    Will be my battle cry
Until I meet my Savior

At my mansion in the sky

17 March 2018

One day, I am going to leave this world and leave all my troubles behind. It will be a glorious day when I get to embrace my Savior at the gates of Heaven. He has prepared for me my own mansion to dwell in. I can hardly wait to get there!

"But as it is, they desire a better country, that is, a heavenly one. Therefore God is not ashamed to be called their God, for he has prepared for them a city" (Hebrews 11:16).

<u>Through Christ</u>

Through Christ I'll face my troubles
    Through Christ I'll face my pain
I will trust my loving Savior
    And never doubt Him again

Through both good and bad times
    I know He's always there
For Christ promised to be with me
    For He will help me through my cares

My life won't always be easy
    Or turn out the way I'd like it to be
But my Faithful, Loving Father
    Always knows what's best for me

So, please forgive me, Father
    For the times that I doubt You
And help me rest on the assurance
    That You will always see me through

2018

    My lovely wife and I have faced many trials
in our marriage and our lives, but we can always

depend on God to give us the strength to see us through. Whatever I face in this world, I know I can turn it over to Christ. I know He loves and cares for me.

> *"I can do all things through Christ who strengthens me"* (Philippians 4:13).

Take Me, Lord

Take me, Lord, and make me, Lord
    And work Your love through me
For I know that I'm the only Gospel
    That others will ever see

Take me, Lord, and make me,
    A vessel of Your Will
Help me to bring Your Gospel
    So other's hearts You will fill

Take me, Lord, and make me
    A person who will pray
For others to come to You
    And to completely follow Your Way

Take me, Lord, and make me
    As one who's sold out to You
And to demonstrate Your love
    In everything I do

14 September 2018

    The Bible tells us that all of God's children need to be willing to share God's love and forgiveness. We need to be ready and willing to be used by God. I wrote this piece to encourage us to be a disciple of God.

"Also I heard the voice of the Lord, saying:
'Whom shall I send, And who will go for Us?'
Then I said, 'Here am I! Send me'" (Isaiah 6:8).

Just Another Day Closer

Just another day closer
    Jesus Christ, my Lord
Just another day closer
    To go to my reward

I know that I'll get there some day
    But I can hardly wait
To see my Lord and Savior
    Waiting at the Golden Gate

Sometimes I get so weary
    Living in this world of sin
But I know I have a purpose here
    And I know that Christ will win

He will keep me 'til I'm done here
    And finish this great race
To share the love of Jesus
    Everywhere and every place

The day is getting closer
    For me to finally go
For me to get to Heaven
    And see the people that I know

I'll wing my way to Jesus
    With my family and my friends
I'll finally be in Paradise
    Where my joy will never end

31 August 2018

I am so looking forward to going to Heaven! Don't get me wrong, I love my life here on this earth. I love my wife and family, all my friends and retirement. However, some days when I get depressed or my body is hurting and not cooperating, I feel so ready to go home to Jesus. I do know that I will be here on earth until my job for Christ is complete.

"But our citizenship is in heaven, and from it we await a Savior, the Lord Jesus Christ, who will transform our lowly body to be like his glorious body, by the power that enables him even to subject all things to himself"
(Philippians 3:20-21).

<u>The Nicest Words</u>

Through all the things I have done in life
    And all that I've been through
The nicest thing anyone has said to me
    Was when she said, "I do"

She agreed to become one with me
    Through good times and through bad
We have had times so joyful
    And other times were sad

I would not change a single thing
    About my awesome wife
She has definitely been a joy to me
    And a blessing in my life

I love you, Nancy, for all you've done
    And have put up with all I've been
Although it's not always easy
    I would do it all again

Heavenly Father, thank You for the girl
    Who became my loving wife
Please bless us and keep us close
    Throughout our earthly life

28 July 2016

"He who finds a wife finds a good thing and obtains favor from the Lord" (Proverbs 18:22).

At the time of this printing, I have been married to the same lovely woman for 39 years. We have raised three children and eight grandchildren, three who are in heaven. I know that I will get to meet them someday!

I like to say that it has not always been easy, but it has always been worth it. With my career in the military, I was gone from home quite a bit and my wife handled everything while I was away. I am grateful we raised our daughter and two sons to be Christians and they are continuing to live it out in their lives and families.

Over the last year, we have faced some serious medical issues, but we are always there to love, support and care for each other. I sincerely do not know what I would do without my wife.

I love you more each day, Nancy! Thank you for being my wife.

<u>One Day</u>

One day my life will be over
    When my work on earth is through
My work for God is finished
    And I've earned the rest that's due

I will lose my earthly body
    And my soul to Heaven will rise
My pain and grief will be over
    When I reach my mansion in the sky

I will reach the gate of Heaven
    And meet our Father and His Son
I cannot wait for them to tell me
    You did a great job Kevin, welcome home

14 March 2017

It is so exciting to know that one day I will leave this world and wake up in the arms of my Jesus. This is so exciting that I can hardly stand it! It is such a blessing to be in the family of God. It is not always calm, I do have my ups, downs and sideways, but no matter what happens I know that I am safe in the Lord.

"So we can confidently say, 'The Lord is my helper; I will not fear; what can man do to me?'" (Hebrews 13:6).

My Body

I wear a mask when I sleep at night
    So, I don't choke and snore
I use a cane when I walk around
    So, I don't hit the floor

My knees hurt and my elbows pain
    And my back is usually sore
My body trembles, I tend to stutter
    My hearing is going bad

Despite all that's going wrong
    I will say, "I'm glad"
To be a child of our Creator
    And His promises that I have

He will guide me and keep me
    As I walk on earth below
And when my body finally gives up
    To Heaven I will go

To dwell with Christ forever
    And to see my family and my friends
I will worship Him forever
    In the land that knows no end!

15 July 2017

I wrote this tongue-in-cheek because everything in this poem is true. It seems that since I retired, my body has a lot more aches and pains. I still remain active, but I have to take it easy.

It is great to know that when I arrive in Heaven, I will have a new body without any ailments or imperfections!

"For we know that if the tent that is our earthly home is destroyed, we have a building from God, a house not made with hands, eternal in the heavens. For in this tent we groan, longing to put on our heavenly dwelling,"
(II Corinthians 5:1-2).

My Reward

One day, I'll pass from this life and go to my reward

    I know I'll go to Heaven because I know the Lord

I'll see my friends and family, and those who've gone before

    But I just want to hear this welcome, from my Lord

Welcome home My child, welcome home My son

    Your time on earth is over, your battle has been won

You served bravely and with honor, and told others about Me

    And now your task is over, and from pain and sin you're free

Come in My lovely child, see the reward I have for you

    Peace and comfort, you will have, in a mansion built for you

You will be in Heaven forever, and will praise your Lord and King

    I want to thank you child, never again will you want for anything

Thank you, my dear child, for what you did for Me

For your suffering and your trials, you had
while serving Me

I love you My dear child and everything that
you've done
So welcome now to Heaven, you're fighting
days are done

11 August 2016

One day, my attempts to serve the Lord will
be rewarded. I know that I am not always the
Christian that God wants me to be and I know
that I disappoint Him at times. But praise Jesus
who died for my sins then rose from the dead
conquering sin and death forever. I am redeemed
through Christ, and one day, He will reward me
for my faithfulness.

*"For we must all appear before the judgment
seat of Christ, so that each one may receive
what is due for what he has done in the body,
whether good or evil"* (II Corinthians 5:10).

My Final Ride

One day, I'll mount upon a bike
    And take my final ride
To my reward in Heaven
    With angels on Gold Wings
Riding by my side

I'll park my bike on streets of gold
    There my Savior will be waiting
To welcome me to my reward
    I run into His arms and say
I love You, thank You, Lord

You have redeemed me from all my sin
    And have always seen me through
All my sadness and temptation
    That this world has put me through
Thank You for bringing me here to my reward
    Thank You for giving me a mansion
Where I can dwell in peace with You
    I will continually praise God and Christ
When my days on earth are through

19 June 2016

There is always a running, light-hearted banter between bike riders about which bike is the best. I myself am partial to the Honda Gold Wing and I have a Gold Wing trike. Our pastor once stated that "Gold Wings are sanctified." Of course, he rides one.

I am so looking forward to going to Heaven and I tell my buddies that I am going to ride my trike on the streets of gold.

"The Lord will rescue me from every evil deed and bring me safely into his heavenly kingdom. To him be the glory forever and ever. Amen"
(II Timothy 4:18).

Innocent Babies

I'll bet the streets of Heaven
 Are lined from wall to wall
With the souls of innocent babies
 Because their parents didn't care at all
These babies could have been great people
 Preachers, Presidents and such
But their lives were snuffed out early
 Because for their parents they were too
  much
They never got a chance to live outside the
 womb
 To grow up and meet new friends
They will never enjoy a sunset
 Or Spring when Winter ends
Their parents made a bad choice
 And it set the baby's souls free
But they are all in Heaven now
 With Jesus they will forever be

October 2015

In my honest opinion, there is no bigger
travesty being practiced in our world today than

the wholesale murder of innocent babies. There have been some new laws recently passed that make it legal to abort a baby up to full term and even after live birth. I know this saddens our Lord.

I used to believe that life begins at conception, but it was recently brought to my attention that I was wrong. Life begins in the mind of God! He is our Creator and has a plan for each of our lives. Abortion takes away the lives of babies who could contribute mightily to our society, but people do not want to take responsibility for their actions or the outcome of their actions.

"Behold, children are a heritage from the Lord, the fruit of the womb a reward. Like arrows in the hand of a warrior are the children of one's youth. Blessed is the man who fills his quiver with them…" (Psalm 127:3-5).

Worried for Our Nation

Lord, we are worried for our nation
 With elections drawing near
We don't know who will get elected
 And for our nation's fate we fear
Lord, we have strayed so far from You
 That's why we are in the shape we are in
We've strayed from our roots, ignore You
 And haughtily continue to sin
Our nation needs to return to You, Lord
 To humble ourself and pray
We need to get back to You
 There is no other way

October 2016

  The year 2016 was a year full of political and societal unrest. The presidential election was to be held in November and our counter was split down the middle in support of their chosen candidate. It was a highly contested election and people on both sides were playing dirty politics for their candidate.

I did not like how either candidate's campaigns were conducted. They were focused on and compounded the other candidate's faults and issues. I have never seen our country in such turmoil and discontent. This is not what our founding fathers envisioned for our country.

"He changes times and seasons; he removes kings and sets up kings..." (Daniel 2:21).

Oh, Father God, We Need You

Oh, Father God, we need You
    There is so much anger in our world
People are angry at their leaders because it is
  not who they wanted
        People are angry at each other for the beliefs
            and convictions they hold
People are angry at You for not being the God
  they want.

Oh, Father God, we need You
    There is so much disrespect in our world
People do not respect others or their property
        People do not respect other's opinions,
            beliefs or even the way they look
People do not even respect themselves
        They don't respect the very way that You
            created them and try to change what You
            have perfectly knit together in their
            mother's womb.

Oh, Father God, we need You
    There is so much hatred in our world
People hate elected officials and hurt, destroy
  and even kill others in their hatred and anger
        People hate others who are different than
            them, they mock, deride, and try to destroy
            them
People hate the very individuals who lay their
  lives on the line every day to protect them

People seem to hate everyone and
themselves.

Oh, Father God, we need You
Your children have failed You
We are fearful to share You with others
We ignore daily readings of Your Word
We ignore opportunities to serve You
We run from occasions to share You
We don't take the time to pray to You
We are too busy to spend time with You
We ignore Your prompting and guidance

Oh, Father God, we need You
We need You to work through us, Your
children
We need You to give us wisdom and courage
We need You to give us power and strength
We need You to prompt us, to prod us into
action
You are the only hope for each of us, for our
country, for Your world.

Please show us what to do, what to say and what
to pray for
Show us who to talk to, who to show love to
Show others how to believe and accept Your
saving grace

Help us to love others as You have loved us
I love You. Amen.

August 2017

The nation was in turmoil before the election, but after the election it increased ten-fold. A portion of our nation became upset because their candidate did not win, and they literally went berserk. They blamed everything and everyone for the election and made sure that everyone knew it.

These people pouted, ranted and raved, and made life miserable for the newly elected candidates and the country has not been the same since. We lost a lot of creditably in the world because of the actions of individuals who were livid at the election results.

"First of all, then, I urge that supplications, prayers, intersessions, and thanksgivings be made for all people, for kings and all who are in high positions, that we may lead a peaceful and quiet life, godly and dignified in every way. This is good, and it is pleasing in the sight of God our Savior," (I Timothy 2:1-3).

A Brand-New Illness

There is a brand-new illness
    From our VP and on down
It reaches every city
    It reaches every town
It's a virtual epidemic
    And it goes from sea to sea
And I have to say, dear people
    It has even affected me

It's called a mental illness
    Because we realize that we sin
And in asking for forgiveness
    We have asked Christ to come in
We depend upon Him daily
    To be our help and guide
And it gives me joy and comfort
    For Him to live inside

So, if I am considered crazy
    For trusting Christ with my life
Then lock me up forever
    And throw the key aside
I will never denounce my Savior
    In all I say or do
And I'll live with Him forever
    Now tell me, how about you?

20 February 2018

Our vice-president in 2017–2021, Mike Pence, is an avowed solid Christian. Some politicians, trying to make him look bad, declared that his faith was an illness. Needless to say, this caused an uproar in the church community and the plan backfired. It made Mike Pence more appealing to the people.

I wrote this piece as my take on the situation.

"But you are a chosen race, a royal priesthood, a holy nation, a people for his own possession, that you may proclaim the excellencies of him who called you out of darkness into his marvelous light" (I Peter 2:9).

<u>Another School Shooting</u>

A shooting at a school has happened
　　And people are going wild
And blaming inanimate objects
　　And it has really got me riled

A hunk of metal can't hurt anything
　　Unless a person picks it up with evil intent
In an evil nefarious way
　　Then it can kill or maim quite a bit

The problem is simple, it is hearts full of sin
　　Who believe they can live without You
Please make our hearts within pure and free
　　from sin
　　And guide us in all that we do

Please, Father, Creator, Almighty God
　　Please bless us where we stand
Help us to follow You and to trust You
　　All across our hurting land

For we know You are the only way
　　For our country to find peace
Please help us to pray for forgiveness
　　We humbly ask on bended knees

We know that we are nothing at all without You
　　And we know that You love us so
Please come back into our country
　　And show us the right way to go

26 February 2018

On February 14, 2018, there was shooting at a high school in Parkland, Florida. There were numerous individuals injured and 17 people killed in the incident. This was just one of several school shootings that occurred in 2018.

This seems to be a continuing problem that keeps manifesting itself across our country. It is sometimes hard to understand the reasoning behind these actions. However, people started blaming the guns right away. It seems that people want to blame everything except the root cause. It could have been an argument with a teacher, bullying or a breakup. Whatever the reason, the issue is the heart of the shooter. Guns cannot load, aim and shoot themselves. There has to be an individual involved.

Stronger gun laws will not solve this issue. Placing guards in the schools will not completely solve the problem. The only way to solve this issue is to change the hearts of man.

"The good person out of his good treasure brings forth good, and the evil person out of his evil treasure brings forth evil" (Matthew 12:35).

<u>Why?</u>

Satan is alive and well and working in our society
    Why, because we let him
We see the wholesale murder of unborn babies
    Yet applaud the laws protecting animals

We see terrible dissent and hatred
    Because people did not get their way
We are constantly bombarded by hatred
    Because we stand up for our faith

Jesus is alive and well and needed in our society
    And we need to share Him
He can heal the broken hearts
    And bring hope back into shattered lives

He will bring love and peace into lives
    He can cure the hatred and dissent
If we will only let Him come into our lives
    Lord, please come back to us and bless us

I love You. Amen.

20 February 2019

95

We constantly see all the evil in our world and wonder why it is happening and how do we stop it. A lot of it has to do with the misplaced priorities in our society. It has turned its back on God, saying that He is not relevant or needed in our lives. The truth is that they do not want to be accountable to a higher power. God's people need to be more vocal, more active and more persistent in sharing His Word.

We cannot combat all the evil present in our world, but we can bring people into Christ's Kingdom and make a difference in somebody's life. Satan has already lost; we just need to be faithful to God.

"Be sober-minded; be watchful. Your adversary the devil prowls around like a roaring lion, seeking someone to devour. Resist him, firm in your faith, knowing that the same kinds of suffering are being experienced by your brotherhood throughout the world"
(I Peter 5:8-9).

The Empty Tomb

The morning itself was glorious
    The sun bright in the sky
But down below, on a lonely road
    Mary Magdalene walked alone

She trod the road so slowly
    With a feeling of deep gloom
For her Master, Friend and Savior
    Was buried in a cold, lonely tomb

She was going to go see Him
    And to pray her sadness away
But when she arrived at Jesus' tomb
    The stone was rolled away!

She picked up her skirt and ran
    To some disciples she knew so well
"His body is gone, they have taken our Lord
    Where He is, I cannot tell"

They all took off and ran to the tomb
    To verify the sight
It was true, there was no body there
    And it gave them a great fright

All that was left was strips of cloth
    That showed where Jesus lay
And they shook their heads in disbelief
    And slowly walked away

Mary Magdalene stayed and cried alone,
    At the side of Jesus' tomb

Suddenly, there were two angels there
    And dispelled all her gloom

He is not here, He rose from the dead
    And will rule in Heaven above
Then she turned around and saw a man there
    Not recognizing the Savior that she loved

Why do you weep, did you lose someone, Mary?
    She said "Rabbani, you're alive is it true?"
Yes, Mary, He said, for I suffered and died
    To pay the price for all sin that was due

The tomb was not opened for Christ to come out
    But so, that people could come in
To see He was truly risen after suffering and dying
    And paying for all our sin

In John 20, read this Bible account
    And know that this is all true
Christ suffered, died, and rose again
    And He did this all for you

31 March 2018

Based on John 20:1-28

Christmas Day is Over

Christmas Day is over
    The presents are all undone
And with the toys that are not broken
    The kids are having fun

The Christmas feast is over
    The dishes washed and put away
The leftovers are in the refrigerator
    To be served again day after day

What about the feelings
    We had on this special day
The love, the joy, the happiness
    Will they too go away?

Christ will keep the joy within us
    His love will see us through
If we keep Him close beside us
    In all we say and do

26 December 2018

    Christmas is one of the most anticipated and celebrated holidays across the world. It is big business for retailers; a time of hustle and bustle trying to find the perfect gift for a loved one and to gather everything needed for a special feast. Children are full of anticipation for what "Santa" will bring them this holiday.

After the day is over, we quickly lose the spirit of the holiday and go back to our lives. If we remember the true reason that we celebrate Christmas, the birth of Jesus Christ, we can celebrate His love, forgiveness and grace all year long!

"And the Word became flesh and dwelt among us, and we have seen his glory, glory as of the only Son from the Father, full of grace and truth" (John 1:14)

Clap-on, Clap-off

Clap-on, clap-off
　It's my worst nightmare
Clap-on, clap-off
　Following me everywhere

I'm staying in this spooky house
　With clap-claps everywhere
And then a creature found me
　And gave me quite a scare

It chased me through the house
　And I was clapping like mad
I was trying to get away from it
　Cause if it caught me, it'll be bad

Lights-on, lights-off
　It really isn't fun
It's really hard to clap-clap
　When you're really trying to run

Clap-on, lit the bedroom lights
　But I fell down the stairs
On-and-off the lights blinked
　When I hit each step, that night

When the porch lights clapped-on
　I headed for the front door
But the creature managed to trip me
　It was laying on the floor

The lights clapped-off
　Then clapped back on

101

Then the creature grabbed me
   Then I knew that I was gone...

Several years ago, our daughter posted
something on Facebook about monsters and clap-
on, clap-off lights. I was inspired and wrote this
poem for her. When she first saw it, she thought
it was something I found on the Internet, but it
was all me.

The Wasps

It was an epic battle
    Known all throughout the land
Between the wasps of the Pitzer's house
    And Kevin the handyman

It started on a summer day
    The temperature was warm
The wasps saw Kevin working
    And then decided to swarm

The wasps flew toward Kevin
    With murderous intent
A few wasps stung poor Kevin
    And down the ladder he went

The wasps celebrated because they thought
    That their war with Kevin was done
But Kevin was smart and soon returned
    With a weapon better than a gun

He sprayed the nest, shot once then twice
    And sent the wasps to their grave
Because wasps can never beat a human
    With a brand-new can of Raid

Three more nests were destroyed the same way
    Before the brave Kevin's work was done
And the war story will spread across the land
    About the wasp battle Kevin has won

Wasps be warned and beware
    Of humans with a can

Or you will regret and wish you had never met
    Sir Kevin, a brave strong man

3 August 2016

One day, I was happily working on siding our house, when I came upon a nest of wasps. As everyone knows, encountering these flying and stinging insects is not a pleasant experience. This meeting was one of those unpleasant situations. They managed to strafe me and get a few painful stings in before I managed to grab my trusty can of Raid and eradicate the colony. The rest is history.

Man Glitter

There is nothing in this world
    That sends my heart all a-flitter
Like working in my shop at home
    And creating some man glitter

When cutting wood, it floats around
    And settles gently to the floor
And on my head, clothes and such
    And makes me want to make more

I must confess it makes a mess
    When strewn out on the floor
I really have to clean myself off
    Before my wife lets me in the door

Our lives can sometimes be a mess
    With sin and evil everywhere
But if we humble ourselves and confess
    Jesus will always be there

So, if you want to go to Heaven
    Ask Jesus into your heart
And He will help you clean up your life
    And give you a brand-new start

I want to thank You, Jesus
    Because of Your sacrifice
I will stand before God sinless
    Because I asked You into my life.

8 August 2016

I simply love building things. I have built an addition on our house, numerous sheds, computer hutch, cradles for our grandchildren, and even some toys. As you can imagine, there is a lot of sawdust floating around when I am in my workshop. The term, "man glitter," came from my friend Oscar De Morris.

When I saw his post about Man Glitter, it immediately took me back to my time as a church janitor. I detested anyone using glitter because it takes quite a lot to clean it up. That made me realize that our lives are a mess and need a lot to clean up all the sins that we commit. The only way to get rid of our sins and be presentable to our sinless God is through the blood of Jesus Christ.

"Purge me with hyssop, and I shall be clean;
wash me, and I shall be whiter than snow"
(Psalm 51:7).

<u>Love Your Neighbor</u>

To love your neighbor as yourself
    Is what the Bible reads
But this command is very hard
    For us to keep indeed

Your neighbor's dog defecates in your yard
    And his cat kills all the birds
And every time you step outside
    You step on bodies and turds

Their parties are loud, their yard is a mess
    Your property value is going down
Your neighbor's house seems to be a blight
    On your entire town

Love your neighbor, treat them well
    Just like Jesus would do
Brighten their world, show the love of Christ
    And the Father will see you through

Love your neighbor as yourself
    Is what the Bible reads
If you keep this command and share God's love
    You will be rewarded indeed.

2 April 2017

"And you shall love the Lord your God with all your heart and with all your soul and with all your mind and with all your strength.' The second is this: 'You shall love your neighbor as yourself.' There is no other commandment greater than these" (Mark 12:30-31).

This is one of the hardest commandments to follow. It does not refer to the people who live next to you; it means the guy who cuts you off on the highway, the people who you work with or sit next to at the movie theatre.

We are not to simply love them, but love them with all our heart, soul, mind, and strength. How can we share the love of our Savior unless we show them first? This is also not just a suggestion but a commandment. It is not only a commandment but is one of the two great commandments. It is a tough thing to love your neighbor, but through Christ, we can do it!

Even So, Come Quickly

Even so, come quickly, Lord Jesus
    For I can hardly wait
To leave this sinful planet
    And reach the Pearly Gate

I'll see You stand there waiting
    As I finally reach that place
Where I will dwell forever
    And behold Your lovely face

There will be no pain or crying there
    No evil and no sin
I can hardly wait to see You
    I love You, God. Amen.

24 March 2018

"He who testifies to these things says, 'Surely I am coming quickly.' Amen. Even so, come, Lord Jesus! The grace of our Lord Jesus Christ be with you all. Amen"
(Revelation 22:20-21 NKJV).

Salvation Through Christ

Throughout this book, you can see the hope that I have in Christ. You too can have this hope and peace in our troubled world. It does not cost anything and will change your life in ways you cannot imagine!

When I was eleven-years-old, I received Christ into my heart at a Vacation Bible School at the Grace Bible Church in New Castle, Pennsylvania. Mr. Abner DeChant explained to me the need that I have for Christ in my life.

Every one of us needs Christ, whether we know it or not, because we are all sinners in God's eyes. *"for all have sinned and fall short of the glory of God,"* (Romans 3:23 NKJV). This means that everyone—you, me and anyone who has ever lived or will live on this planet—is a sinner, except for Jesus Christ. He is the perfect Son of God.

No sinner can ever face the perfect God and Creator because of our sin. In fact, the Bible tells us, *"For the wages of sin is death, but the gift of God is eternal life in Christ Jesus our Lord"* (Romans 6:23 NKJV). We all deserve to die for our sins and to spend an eternity without Christ. However, there is only one way to be saved from this.

"that if you confess with your mouth the Lord Jesus and believe in your heart that God has

raised Him from the dead, you will be saved.
For with the heart one believes unto
righteousness, and with the mouth confession is
made unto salvation" (Romans 10:9-10 NKJV).

All you need to do to obtain salvation is to say a simple prayer. "Father, I know I am a sinner. I know I do not deserve mercy from You, except through Jesus Christ. I realize that He took all my sin upon Himself and suffered and died to pay the penalty for my sin. I accept that Christ died, was buried and rose triumphantly from the grave to conquer sin and death forever. Please come into my heart and let Jesus be the Lord of my life. Thank You for loving and caring for me. Amen."

Have you prayed this prayer? Are you ready to face life with the power of God with you? I pray that you have and the angels in Heaven are rejoicing, another sinner has come home!

If you have any questions, feel free to contact me at kboaz2001@yahoo.com. I will do the best I can to help you. Blessings to you!

Kevin M. Pitzer
Knight of the Cross

I Will Lay Me Down in Peace

When all life's storm clouds gather round me
    Earthly troubles everywhere,
I know You, Lord, are the One and Only,
    Who knows all my worldly care

Chorus:
And I will lay me down in peace and sleep,
    For I know, Lord, You are there,
To makest me dwell in safety, Lord
    And cover me with Your care

I know I need to trust You fully, Lord
    For Satan is always there,
To tempt me, try me and load me down,
    With burdens too heavy to bear

Chorus

Though Satan attacks me one on one,
    And temptations are always there,
I know the battle is already won,
    Because I know, Lord, You are there

Chorus

When my life's work is finally over,
    And my troubles and cares are gone
I know that I'll forever abide
    With my Savior, God's only Son

Chorus

1998

Psalm 4:8 (KJV), *"I will both lay me down in peace, and sleep: for thou, Lord, only makest me dwell in safety,"* gives us a good message of trusting the Lord no matter what happens and resting safely in His loving arms.

This was my mother's favorite Bible verse. She took it as her life's verse. It has an excellent message. God's people may have a rough life and things may not always go well, but we can rest in the assurance that God is keeping us safe in His arms. If God is for us, who can stand against us?

I dedicate this to my parents, Donald P. & Vivian J. Pitzer, whose Godly upbringing brought me to where I am in my faith today.

He Died on the Cross for Me

For years and years, I wandered
    Down the wide path called sin's road
I did not have a Savior
    To bear my sin-filled load
But then I met my Jesus
    Who bore my sins away
When He died on the cross for me

Chorus:
Oh, He died on the cross for me
    He suffered to set me free
Though my life was filled with sin
    With His love, He took me in

When He died on the cross for me
    He came to earth as a human
To show His love for man
    But they killed Him on Mount Calvary
For they did not understand
    But He rose up from the grave
Over death a victory
    When He died on the cross for me

Chorus

And now I'm walking daily
    Down the straight and narrow road
And though I often struggle
    He is there to bear my load
I know He will be with me
    Throughout eternity

For He died on the cross for me

Chorus

29 September 1998

I honestly do not remember what prompted me to write this song, but it is a reminder of what Jesus went through for us to save us from sin. The least I can do for Him is to live my life bringing glory to His name.

This Could Be the Day

When I wake up in the morning
    With my sleep still on my face
I look at the world around me
    And think I want to leave this place
I just thank my Savior always
    For saving me from sin
And I know without a doubt
    My heavenly reservations are in

Chorus:
Oh, this could be the day
    When my Jesus comes to say
"I will take you to our home so far away!"
    He will take me by the hand
And lead me to the Promised Land
    Oh, this could be that day
That very day!

When I break for lunch at midday
    O Lord, please help me get through
The temptations all around me
    I want to live my life for You
Want to be a testimony
    To all those that I see
Cause I know at any moment
      My Jesus could come down for me

Chorus

When I lay my head on my bed
    Before I close my eyes to sleep

I think of those who don't know You
    And I almost want to weep
Lord, help me to be a witness
    To show Your love and care
So, when I get to Heaven
    My friends will already be there

2002

Lay Your Burdens on Down

Lay your burdens on down,
　　At the foot of the cross,
Where Jesus suffered and died,
　　He gave His life at great loss.

Lay your burdens on down,
　　Christ will take them all away,
And your journey will be brighter,
　　And your load will be much lighter,
Cause Jesus Christ will take them all away.

2004

You Can't Buy Your Way to Heaven

You can't buy your way into Heaven,
   Paying cash for your reward,
You can't do good works your whole life,
   And expect to meet the Lord.

You cannot reach those pearly gates,
   Just because you go to church,
Cause if you depend on these things,
   You'll find yourself in a lurch.

Chorus:
Cause the only way to Heaven,
   Is through Jesus Christ the Lord,
Just accept Him into your heart,
   You're on the way to your reward,
Just follow Jesus faithfully,
   And soon you'll begin to see,
That the only way to Heaven,
   Is as easy as can be.

Master Card and Visa and Discover will reject,
   For God's in "charge" of everything,
So, what did you expect?
   Debit cards will be useless,
ATM's will not be there,
   American Express and traveler's checks,
Won't work at all up there.

Chorus

119

Gold bullion and silver ingots,
    Just will not cut it, my man,
The only "Diner's Club" up there,
    Is the Marriage Feast of the Lamb,
Lay up your treasures in Heaven,
    In the bank that can't be robbed,
So, when you leave and go to Heaven,
    You'll inherit the riches of God.

Chorus

2004

My Air Force Reserve unit at Grissom Air Reserve Base was conducting all their operations out of Wright Patterson Air Force Base during the summer of 2004 because our runway at home was undergoing major repairs. One evening while my vehicle was in the shop being repaired, I decided to walk to an Italian restaurant for dinner. It was a long walk, almost two miles. On the way back, I started thinking, "Some people think that just by going to church and putting money into the offering will get them into Heaven." Our society nowadays are so materialistic and focused on money that they think money will get them anything.

It is meant to be a lighthearted song, with a serious message.

In Matthew 6:19-20, Christ tells us, *"Do not lay up for yourselves treasures on earth, where moth and rust destroy and where thieves break in and steal; but lay up for yourself treasures in heaven, where neither moth nor rust destroys and where thieves do not break in and steal."*

No matter how much money or how many possessions someone has, they cannot but their way into Heaven. Only a humble spirit, depending on a relationship with God will get you there. The only way to get into Heaven is through a relationship with Jesus Christ.

11 January 2005

His Great Love for Me

I sit here and marvel
    At His great love for me
He was beaten and bruised
    And He suffered and died
For this lowly sinner, me

His amazing love so boundless
    Has taken away my sin
And all that He asks in return
    Is that I live for Him

His blessings reach me every day
    In me He does abide
Though troubles and trials beset me
    He is always by my side

And when my life is over
    He will take me by the hand
To Heaven's delight, in a mansion bright
    I'll live in Glory Land

I want to thank You, Jesus
    For Your great love for me
How You were beaten and bruised
    And You suffered and died
For a sinner, which is me

23 August 2004 ©2006
Flying somewhere between Hawaii and Japan

122

I worked full time as a civilian for the United States Air Force Reserve; my part time job was in the Air Force Reserves. In my job as an aircraft mechanic, I had the opportunity to fly all over the world on the KC-135R aircraft, which I worked on.

August 2004 found me on a medical run from California to Hawaii to Japan and back. There was a lot of flying on these missions, and we had a lot of time to kill during the flights. I was laying down in my cot when this song came to me. I immediately got up and wrote it down before I forgot it.

Jesus Christ died on the cross for each one of us. He took upon Himself the sins of everyone who has lived and who will ever live. Jesus wants us to depend on Him in all we do. He wants us to give Him all our worries and cares. As a man, it is hard for us to give these things up, but if we fully trust in Him, our life would be so much easier.

11 January 2005

<u>The Mighty Men of God</u>

Dedicated to Rev. Carroll VanAnda
January 19, 1926 – August 3, 2003

Dedicated to Pastor Jerry M. Moore
March 12, 1960 – March 8, 2022

They go bravely into battle
    With the Bible as their sword
They fight the devil daily
    Bringing lost souls to the Lord
They are faithful, fruitful, humble,
    Loving, kind, and true
Remember that these men of God
    Also pray and care for you

Chorus:
These men are on the front line
    In a battle every day
They have dedicated their lives
    To keep the enemy at bay
They are walking on the pathway
    That those before have trod
They are our faithful pastors
    The mighty men of God

You will find them in the churches
    Spread all across this land
You will find them in the hospitals
    Holding a sick one's hand
You will find them praying quietly

Beside the dying one's bed
You will find these men wherever
    The hand of God has led

They are standing in the background
    The pastor's family and his wife
Missed baseball games and dinners
    Are common in their life
But they keep on standing faithfully
    Knowing their loved one's call
And knowing though he's not always there
    He deeply loves them all

Let us not forget our pastor
    In his duties, every day
And always remember faithfully
    For him and his family to pray
Support this man in all you can
    And help to ease his load
And walk beside him every day
    As he travels this lonesome road

31 August 2004

    I have always had a healthy respect for
pastors and how difficult their jobs are. My best

friend, Jerry Moore, was a youth pastor at our church for nine years. I worked really closely with him and saw all the unique problems that came with the territory.

October is Pastor Appreciation Month and I felt I should write something with that in mind. It took a while to get it started, but once I did, the words just flowed.

As soon as we got back to Ohio, I typed the song up on the computer and emailed it to my wife with instructions to let our church secretary/organist, Mary K. Johnson, look at it and see if it was worth putting music to.

Mary worked hard on the music and had it ready for October. The choir was scheduled to sing it on the last Sunday of the month. Of course, I was on alert that day and was not supposed to leave base, but my good friend, John Meier, gladly took over for me so I could be at church when the choir sang my song. I tell you that is a weird feeling to sit in a pew and hear the choir sing the words that God gave me to honor our pastors.

11 January 2005

Moving on With Jesus

Life's journey here on earth always has its ups
and downs,
> Sometimes we feel so joyful; sometimes we
> wear a frown,
But if we trust in Jesus, He will guide us on our
way,
> Then we can stand in front of the world, and
> from our hearts we say,

Chorus:
We are moving on with Jesus, thru life's
pathways we trod,
> We are moving on with Jesus, living out our
> lives for God.
We are moving on with Jesus, as He takes us by
our hand,
> We are moving on with Jesus, to His
> Precious Promised Land.

There are trials and tribulations and there are
always woes and cares,
> But one thing we can count on, Jesus will
> always be there.
He will love, comfort and guide us through
whatever's in our way,
> Then we will thank Him, praise Him and
> love Him as we go on our way.

Chorus

Life's not always a trial; there will be happiness, joy and love,
> And God will always reward us with
> blessings from above.
Fellowship with other Christians, our families and our friends,
> We will have the peace that Jesus gives us,
> and we can say again,

Chorus

We have our time upon this earth, but it will soon come to an end,
> If we can say without a doubt, that Jesus was
> our friend,
We will look back on the journey and thank Jesus on that day,
> Because we can stand in front of God and
> with grateful hearts can say,

Chorus

9 January 2005

    I sent a copy of my song *"The Mighty Men of God"* to my mother-in-law, Bernice VanAnda, because I dedicated it to her late husband,

Reverend Carroll VanAnda, who had passed away from bone cancer in August 2003. She liked the song so well that she called me in the night of January 7, 2005, asking me to write a song about moving around here on earth. Being a pastor's wife, they moved around quite a bit throughout their calling.

The evening before I was working in my shop, cutting wood on my radial arm saw, and managed to cut two of my fingers. This resulted in a trip to the emergency room, where I got prescriptions for antibiotics and pain.

When she called, I had just taken a pain pill. Rather than making me drowsy, I really got wound up. After going to bed, my mind and body would just not stop working, so I could not get to sleep. While I was lying there, the phrase "Moving on With Jesus" came to me, and the chorus started to take shape.

Since I could not sleep, I got up and started typing the chorus on the computer, and the rest just flowed out. At 2am Sunday morning, I finished the song and emailed it to Bernice. I called her much later that morning and told her to check her email.

She called back a few minutes later and was extremely pleased with the lyrics. But she laughed and said, "You did not have to write it within 24 hours!" She called back the next night with another song idea, but I have not started that one yet.

I like the philosophy of life that says, "Life is like a roll of toilet paper, the closer you get to the end, the faster it goes." Life is a journey. It is sometimes pleasant and happy, but there are always bumps and detours along the way. Those of us who have a relationship with Jesus will always have Him walking beside us to help us along the way. As I like to say, working for Jesus does not always pay well, but the retirement is out of this world!

11 January 2005

Take My Life, Lord Jesus

Take my life, Lord Jesus
    I give it all to you
I know I've made a mess of it
    But I know what You can do

Take my heart, Lord Jesus
    I know it's full of sin
I confess it all to you, Lord
    Please make me pure within

Take my mind, Lord Jesus
    And clean the evil out
I want to live a life for You
    Where people have no doubt

I love and thank You, Jesus
    For dying on that tree
You sacrificed Your precious life
    And You did it all for me

Jesus, walk beside me
    And guide me on the way
I know You will be beside me
    And be with me all my days

18 February 2005

When we accept Christ into our lives, we accept Him with our whole self, mind, body, and soul. We need to die daily to sin and serve Christ in all that we do.

I am a Christian, but that does not make me perfect. I am a sinner, and I need to confess my sins daily and fully depend on God to guide me throughout my life.

21 February 2005

Oh, I Want to Be in Heaven

I've got a mansion up in Heaven
    With a lawn, all trimmed and neat
I've got a crown to place upon my head
    As I walk down that golden street
There will be no sin, no tears
    No crying, pain, or care
And the best thing about it all
    Christ will be everywhere

Chorus:
Heaven is the only place I really want to be
    Where my Christian friends and family will
        be there to welcome me
Where my Loving Savior, Jesus, will be waiting
    at the gate
        Yes, I want to be in Heaven
Oh, I can hardly wait

Oh, how we will worship Jesus there
    And to thank Him for His love
What a blessed, glorious time of praise
    For all the blessings from above
For Christ, Himself laid down His life
    To save us all from sin
Oh, friend it is not too late
    Oh, won't you let Him come in

Chorus

I want to pass through those Pearly Gates
    With the fellowship so grand

Where Christ is blessed with glory, love and
  praise
    All across the Heavenly Land
The best church service ever
    Will always be going on there
And Christ Himself will be the one
    To lead the service there

Chorus

As much as I enjoy life here on earth with my lovely wife, our children and all our friends, Heaven is the place I want to be. I know my wife and children will join me there and my parents are already waiting on me, along with many Christian friends I have known throughout the years.

Heaven will be eternal joy and peace in the presence of Jesus. There will be no grass to cut or bills to pay, just eternal fellowship with Christ and all the saints.

I can hardly wait!

21 February 2005

In the Twinkling of an Eye

I may be driving down the road
    Or outside cutting grass
I don't know when my time will come
    And I will breathe my last
But I can always be assured
    With Jesus by my side
I'm gladly looking forward to
    That happy Heavenly ride

Chorus:
In the Twinkling of an eye, Lord
    I'll be soaring through the air
In the Twinkling of an eye, Lord
    There will be no pain or care
In the Twinkling of an eye, Lord
    Your glory will shine anew
In the Twinkling of an eye, Lord
    I will dwell forever with You

All of us who love the Savior
    Will be transformed in a flash
With the trump of God resounding
    We will be home at last
We'll be dressed in robes of glory
    Our light will always shine
We'll forever tell the story
    Praise God, Jesus is mine

Chorus

Oh, come quickly now, Lord Jesus

We long to be with You
But our work may not be finished
So, work for You we'll do
But our reward will be waiting
It's coming by and by
And we'll dwell with you forever
And reign with you on high

21 February 2005

"In a moment, in the twinkling of an eye, at the last trump: for the trumpet shall sound, and the dead shall be raised incorruptible, and we shall be changed" (I Corinthians 15:52 KJV).

I simply love the concept that we will be changed in the "twinkling of an eye." One second, we will be living out our daily lives and before we can blink, we will be in the presence of Jesus.

I was sitting in church when the chorus came to mind. I furiously scribbled it on the back of my bulletin before I forgot it. I later showed the chorus to my family and my daughter said that she wondered what I was writing down on the bulletin.

There are times when I am ready to go, but Jesus has plans for our lives that we do not know about. All we can do is wait patiently and continue to do His will as we await our reward.

21 February 2005

My Last Goodbye

Dedicated in Memory of Sheila Purcell

The Lord brought us together so many years ago
    The years just seemed to fly by as our love
    continued to grow
It wasn't always easy; life is not a joy ride
    But we always had each other, with Jesus by
    our side

I feel so lonely, Father, I really want to cry
    But You will still be with me
As I say my last goodbye
    My life on earth must still go on
And with me You will abide
    I wouldn't make it Jesus
Without You by my side

The angels came and took you sweetheart to a
land that knows no tears
    You will have a perfect body, one that will
    know no fears
Someday I'll come to join you and in Heaven
we'll abide
    And we will always be together, with Jesus
    by our side
Our children and grandchildren, how they gave
us such joy
    And how we loved and prayed for each little
    girl and boy

Though they will all be lonely, in peace they can abide
　　Knowing you are up in Heaven with Jesus
　　by your side
Lord, as You take my beloved to dwell with You above
　　I know that death cannot break our precious
　　bonds of love
One day, I'll come to join her, and we will walk hand in hand
　　To be with You forever in Heaven's Glory
　　Land

26 February 2005

　　The world lost a great lady of faith on 26 February 2005. Sheila Purcell had undergone major surgery about a week before her passing. She served with our pastor at our church for over 18 years. Her passing was sudden and shocked the whole church and community. I have never been to a church service like the one we had the day after her passing. Walking into the church that morning was like walking into a funeral home. Everyone was talking in whispers and with the music playing it was a little bit eerie.

When the service started, Kent Spence, our head deacon, explained about Sheila's passing and described how good of a mood she was in on that afternoon. My best friend, Jerry Moore, our former youth pastor, gave the sermon. It was an uplifting sermon showing us that even though the church is going through a tough time right now, Jesus is walking beside each one of us all the way. It was a blessing for the whole church.

My wife, family and I had a rough weekend to start out with. Nancy had to take our oldest boy, Aaron, to the emergency room at 3:00 a.m. Friday morning with chest pains. Me, being on alert, did not know about it until I made my daily call home about 7:00 a.m. I rushed from work to the hospital. Apparently, he somehow got a hole in his bronchial tube and filled his lung and heart cavity with air. So, my wife and I spent most of the day Friday and Saturday at the hospital. Warren Purcell stopped by Friday morning to see Aaron and to pray with us. I asked him about Sheila, and he said she was doing fine and should be home this weekend.

I called my sister on Friday morning to let her know what was happening with Aaron and found out her husband was in the hospital with some heart problems.

Saturday night, my wife and I were exhausted. It is surprising how much having a kid in the hospital wears you out. We went to bed early and were sleeping when my daughter told us about the phone call she received about Sheila. When Jessalyn knocked on our door that late at night, I got goose bumps before she told us. A lot goes through your mind in that short period of time.

After receiving the news, it was hard to sleep, so I got up and wrote this song in memory of Shelia. It was difficult to write because of the love and dedication that goes into a marriage of that many years, especially with the unique stresses of a pastor's life. I knew it would be so hard to say goodbye to somebody who you have lived with and loved for so many years. But as Christians, we know we will be reunited with our loved ones in Heaven.

28 February 2005

The Great Makeover

Some people say I'm different and people think
   I'm strange
But I can't wait to get to Heaven and get my
   body rearranged
My ear hair will move north to my scalp where
   it belongs
And my belly fat will move to my arms and
   make me look so strong
My aches and pains will disappear, and all my
   teeth will shine
Oh, I can't wait to get to Heaven for my great
   makeover time!

Chorus:
For my Lord will make me over, a new body
   without pain
And I will have all my teeth and hair and
   hearing once again
No nips and tucks will be needed, just a
   twinkling from God's eye
And I'll be transformed forever at my makeover
   in the sky

Oh, when I get to Heaven, I'll wear robes of
   purest white
My face will be so handsome, unlike now it
   gives a fright
I'll have a full head of hair without one out of
   place
My teeth will be bright and even without one

extra space
My warts and moles will disappear, my
  suffering will be over
When I get to Heaven and have my great
  makeover

The older I get on this earth, the more my body
  falls apart
Bad breath and eyes and hearing are a few for
  just a start
My behind and belly are getting big, my
  bladder's getting small
And if I don't stand up carefully, I know I'm
  bound to fall
My back goes out more than I do and I'm no
  longer tall
But I can't wait to get to Heaven for the greatest
  makeover of all

There will be no need for liposuction,
  enhancements or even Nair
Botox and enlargements will not matter cause
  people just won't care
We will be in the presence of Jesus, and in His
  light, we will shine
We will be praising the Father, the Creator of us
  all
There will be no need for plastic surgeons
  constantly on call
Because Christ Himself will give us the greatest
  makeover of them all

5 March 2005

Even So, Come Quickly, Jesus

Even so, come quickly, Jesus
    For I can hardly wait
Until I find myself in Heaven
    Walking through those Pearly Gates
I want to wrap my arms around You
    And give You a big hug
For You suffered and died to save me
    Your act of ultimate love

2005

I do not know when I wrote this song or what the circumstances were, but I found the folded paper with the song written down in my handwriting.

I feel this song summarizes the hope of all believers, to go to Heaven and meet Jesus, who sacrificed so much for us.

Thank You, Jesus, for the hope You give us.

"He which testifieth these things saith, Surely I come quickly. Amen. Even so, come, Lord Jesus" (Revelation 22:20 KJV).

8 October 2005

Hang On

The disciples were so lonely
    Their Savior had just died
On that cruel cross at Calvary
    It made them want to cry
But in a flash of blinding light
    Christ in front of them stood
"Do not be afraid, my friends
    I have a promise for you"
He said…

Chorus:
Hang on just a little bit longer and I'll come
  back for you
    Hang on just a little bit longer
And all your troubles and trials will be through
    No longer will you roam
Cause Heaven will be your grand and glorious
  home
    Just hang on just a little bit longer and I'll be
      back for you

The Christians on this earth wait
    For Christ to come again
We daily fight life's battles
    And temptation from sin
We keep our hearts in the Bible
    And our eyes turned toward the sky
If we listen to the wind carefully
    We will hear our Savior sigh
If you…

Chorus

When you accept the Savior
    Into your heart to stay
He promises to be there with you
    And to keep you day to day
And when your life is over
    And your work down here is through
When you are ready to reap your reward
    The Lord will softly say to you
If you…

Chorus

My soul is getting restless
    As I lay here in this bed
It wants to go to Heaven
    Visions of glory fill my head
As I lay here softly praying
    I let out a soft sigh
I heard my Savior tell me
    Your time is drawing nigh
So just…

Chorus

8 November 2005

Come Unto the Father

Come to Him little sister
    Who is living on the street
She has to sell her body
    Just to get some food to eat
I know you are feeling weary
    Overwhelmed with sin
Oh, please come to the Father
    He wants to take you in

Chorus:
Oh, come unto the Father
    He wants to take you in
His arms are open wide
    To take away your sin
He wants to show He loves you
    Your burdens He will set free
And when your life is over
    You'll live with Him eternally

Oh, brother in the bar room
    To hide your sin and shame
You cheated on your dear wife
    And destroyed your family name
The Father will forgive you
    And help you with your shame
Oh, please come to the Father
    He loves us all the same

Chorus

To you who are listening

147

To this provoking song
One day, your life will be over
It may be short or long
No sin that you've committed
Will decrease the Father's care
Oh, please come to the Father
Your burdens He will share

Chorus

18 November 2005

A Brand-New Address

My home here on earth is temporary
    I'll be here just a little while
When I think of my next home
    It makes me start to smile
I'll have a glorious mansion
    Beside a crystal sea
Christ built this habitation
    Especially for me

Chorus:
I've got a brand-new address
    Upon a golden street
I'll have my Heavenly crowns
    To cast at Jesus' feet
All my neighbors will be loved ones
    Who have gone on before
I just can't wait to walk through
    My Heavenly mansion's door

I will need no moving company
    Or even a pick-up truck
Cause when I get to Heaven
    I won't need this earthly stuff
My mansion will be furnished
    With things, I can't conceive
Oh, when I think of Heaven
    I can hardly wait to leave

Chorus

My Mom and Dad will meet me

149

At the Pearly Gates
And Christ Himself will take me
To my new dwelling place
It will be a grand reunion
At Resurrection Square
And Christ and all His angels
Will lead the party there

Chorus

18 November 2005

We Have the Victory

Oh, Hades where is your triumph
    Oh, death where is your sting
Christians have victory over you
    By the Blood of Christ, the King
We remain steadfast and immovable
    Our labor is not in vain
We wait and pray and look to the sky
    For Christ to come again
We reach out to lost souls constantly
    As daily for them we pray
For them to meet the Savior
    Some glorious life-changing day
For we are changed by Christ Himself
    To bring lost souls to the Lord
And when we go to live with Christ
    Great will be our reward
So, Christians talk to your fellow man
    To bring them to the Lord
They too can bring their friends to Christ
    According to His Word
All together we can thank the Lord
    And forever His praises sing
For He has triumphed over Hades
    And removed from death its sting

30 November 2005

Exhort Your Fellow Christians

Exhort your fellow Christians
    Into your life take them in
For it could be your loving presence
    That keeps them from some great sin
Encourage your fellow Christians
    Through their life from day to day
You could be a tremendous blessing
    Through what you do or say
Pray for your fellow Christians
    It is what the Lord wants us to do
And through all the trials and tribulations
    The Lord will see us through
Live to make more fellow Christians
    Keep working for the Lord
If you remain true and faithful
    Great will be your reward
Christ will bless all His children for loving and
    serving Him

17 December 2005

Listen for the Sound of the Golden Trumpet

We are waiting with anticipation
      For the Second Coming of the Lord
It's a promise that He has given us
      Cause it's written in His Holy Word
We can't wait for the skies to open
      And Jesus descending with His Holy band
All of us Christians will be glad to rise
      And start living in God's Glory Land

We want to...

Chorus:
Listen for the sound of the golden trumpet
      It means Christ has come back again
All the dead in Christ will rise
      Then His saints will rise to be with Him
All His children will dwell in Heaven's glory
      Giving praise to the Holy Lamb
So, listen for the sound of the golden trumpet
      And the coming of the great "I AM"

We can see the signs of His coming
      Hate and unrest throughout the land
Wars and battles being fought all over
      And man being evil to man
Earthquakes, tsunamis, hurricanes, and
   volcanoes driving people from their homes
      Are just another sign of His coming
Cause the earth is beginning to groan

153

Make sure you...

Chorus

So here is a warning to all of you sinners
    You need to get this into your mind
You better give up sinning and turn to Christ
    Or you will surely be left behind
Just confess your sins to Jesus
    And invite Him into your heart
Then He will always walk beside you
    And the wonderful blessings will start

Then you can...

Chorus

6 January 2006

God Is on His Throne

Do you feel discouraged?
    Do you feel alone?
Do not be disheartened
    For God is on His throne
If you come to Him humbly
    With a sincere heartfelt prayer
He will guide you through your troubles
    He will always be there

February 2006
Keflavik, Iceland

<u>The Valley</u>

I've walked through the valley, Lord
    Without You by my side
I felt so scared and lonely
    I had no place to hide
But then I met You, Jesus
    You gladly took me in
You led me through the valley, Lord
    And took away my sin
I thank You for the valleys, Lord
    For without them how would I know
That no matter how deep and long they are
    I have a place to go
For You are always waiting
    To walk and guide me through
For if it wasn't for You, Jesus
    I don't know what I would do

February 2006
Keflavik, Iceland

I Just Want to be a Blessing

I just want to be a blessing
    As I live from day to day
So, my friends will see Christ in me
    In everything I do or say
I just want to be a blessing
    So that everyone will see
That I have the living Savior
    Christ alive and living in me!

<u>Bright Hope</u>

Our world is full of anger
    Hate, discontent, and scorn
Sometimes I start to wonder
    Why is this going on?
Then I stop and remember
    Just who is in control
It is Christ Almighty
    The Savior of my soul

Chorus:
We have a bright hope for the future
    With Jesus Christ, our Lord
He will always be beside us
    It's written in His Word
Just ask the Living Savior
    Into your heart today
You'll have the bright hope right beside you
    As you live from day to day

We know that in the future
    Christ will take His children home
We will dwell with Him in Heaven
    And worship at His Throne
There will be no pain or crying
    All will be peaceful there
And Christ, our ray of bright hope
    Will be our ruler there

Chorus

11 September 2006

158

My family and I visited my siblings in Pennsylvania over Labor Day weekend. While there, we visited my sisters' church, Bright Hope Community Church, in Butler, Pennsylvania. It was there that I conceived the idea for a song about bright hope. A few days later, I wrote out the words to the chorus.

Sitting in my office on September 11, 2006, there was a constant stream of radio spots in remembrance of 9-11, 2001. I was thinking that this country and the whole world needs to know about the bright hope we have in Christ. I then wrote the verses to the song, hopefully sharing the need of revival in our land.

He Walked Upon the Water

He walked upon the water
    Changed water into wine
He made the dead to live again
    And He saved this soul of mine
He healed the brokenhearted
    The crippled and the lame
And praise the Lord, Halleluiah
    He's coming back again

Chorus:
Oh, Jesus, Jesus, Jesus
    The Savior of my soul
He healed my sad and broken heart
    And He made my spirit whole
Oh, Jesus, Jesus, Jesus
    A never-ending friend
And Praise the Lord, Halleluiah
    He's coming back again!

My soul was lost and weary
    Of sin, anger and pain
I was headed down the wrong path
    No peace there would I gain
But then I met my Savior
    He took my sins away
And Praise the Lord, my Savior
    Walks beside me all the way

Chorus

The day Christ died upon the cross

He took away our sin
But then He rose on the third day
    Old Satan could not win
Christ now lives up in Heaven
    Where there are no tears or pain
If you love and serve the Savior
    You will dwell forever with Him

Chorus

June to September 2007

This song developed over a period of a couple of months. I wrote down the basic concept of the song and built on it from there. I thought on it and wrote a good portion of it while I was deployed to Turkey.

I thought and thought about it and finally got the last two verses written down. I started the song in May and finally finished it in September.

It is so exciting to be on God's side. There is so much that He can do for us if we only ask Him and have faith in Him.

God Wants to Talk to You

If you listen closely, way deep inside of you
    You will hear a still small voice
God wants to talk to you
    You won't hear Him through an earthquake
Or in a mighty rushing wind
    Just go off alone and humble yourself
Just sit and talk with Him

If you break away from your busy life
    To go find a quiet place
To pour out your heart to the Father
    You will find an inner peace

God wants to help and guide you
    As you walk down life's rugged road
He wants to share your burdens
    And lift your heavy load
All you must do is ask Him
    Get on your knees and pray
And God will walk beside you
    Every night and every day

God wants to help and guide you
    As you walk down life's rugged road
He wants to share your burdens
    And lift your heavy load
All you must do is ask Him
    Get on your knees and pray
And God will walk beside you
    Every night and every day

I Have Beautiful Feet

I have beautiful feet, beautiful feet
 They keep me walking down the street
To tell everyone I happen to meet
 About the sweet, sweet love of God

I have beautiful eyes, beautiful eyes
 I see friends, grass, trees, moon, and skies
All of creation helps me realize
 The sweet, sweet love of God

I have beautiful ears, beautiful ears
 So that I can sit still and hear
What teachers and preachers have to tell me
 About the sweet, sweet love of God

I have a beautiful heart, beautiful heart
 Where Christ is living in every part
I want to know; I'm filled head to toe
 With the sweet, sweet love of God

2007

We're Sleeping with a Harley

We rode into the campground
    With no place to lay our head
Our friends said, "Come on over,"
    And offered us a bed.
"You can sleep inside our camper,
    In the garage beside our bike."
So, we went with them, and thanked them,
    Hoping things would work out right.

So, we're sleeping with a Harley,
    And there's oil on my pillow
When you're sleeping with a Harley,
    It doesn't snore, it bellows
Our stress level is peaking,
    Because we are not sleeping,
We're sleeping with a Harley,
    And we're scared.

My Gold Wing is sitting outside
    Alone among the stars
There is nothing parked beside it
    Not a truck or even a car
I know it's feeling lonely
    May even start to sigh.
And if I know my Gold Wing
    It may even start to cry

Because we're sleeping with a Harley,
    And there's oil on my pillow
When you're sleeping with a Harley,

164

It doesn't snore, it bellows
Our stress level is peaking,
    Because we are not sleeping,
We're sleeping with a Harley,
    And we're scared.

But it's not about where you're sleeping
    Or about your favorite bike
It's all about great friendships
    That want to be Christ-like
So, help each other when you can
    And show them that you care
That way we can spread the love
    Of Jesus, everywhere.

So, we're sleeping with a Harley
    And we don't really care
Because our fellow CMAers
    Were really glad to share
So, be nice to your neighbors
    Be a blessing to your friends
For you will be rewarded
    By Jesus, in the end

May 2013

My wife and I are part of a great Christian motorcycle group, The Christian Motorcyclist's Association. Our state rally in 2013 was held at Camp Camby, IN. We were hesitant to go because all the rooms were already reserved, and we would have to stay in a hotel.

I was talking to one of our members, Rich Harlan, and he said that they were taking their toy hauler down and were staying in it, but we would be more than welcome to sleep in their camper's garage. He then told me the only downside to sleeping there was that we would have to sleep with his Harley, ribbing us because we ride a Honda Gold Wing.

I got to thinking it would make a great country music song, and "We're Sleeping with a Harley" was born.

A Life That is Lived for Jesus

A life that is lived for Jesus
    Will have blessings that come from above
One of these blessings that I treasure the most
    Is my life with the one that I love

Life on this earth is not easy
    It is filled with sunshine and pain
But as long as I have my sweet Nancy
    I would do it all over again

Our lives we have shared together
    Has been a blessing to me I know
Because God gave me a wonderful woman
    Whose love for me always shows

Through many long and short separations
    With my job when I was away
To each other we remained faithful
    We would have it no other way

We have had some really tough problems
    But with the Lord and our church at our side
We have always managed to overcome them
    And remain happy husband and bride

We've raised our three children to trust God
    And we can be proud of each one
God blesses the family that loves Him
    And worships together as one

So, I want to thank you sweet Nancy
    For the happiness that you've given me

I love you so much that I want to
    Be with you for eternity

When one accepts Christ as their Savior, they become a Child of God. This does not automatically make their life easy and painless, but God will give His children gifts, in the form of blessings.

The best thing that ever happened to me in my life, except my salvation, was when God gave me my sweet Nancy to be my wife. This coming June, on Flag Day, we will be married for 25 years. I am so blessed with this in many ways.

It has not always been easy for us. We have been through some tough times, but it has all been worth it. It is so good to come home from work to a warm hug. I have been away a lot with my job, and that has not been easy on Nancy, but with a faithful God and a loving church to support us, everything has worked out.

We have raised three children who each have a loving relationship with God. They have never gotten into trouble at school or in the community. They daily show their love for God and their family. I know our family is a minority in this society, a biological family living under one roof, but that just proves that God still cares for His children.

It is a real blessing to me because Nancy has stood by me for 25 years. I have not always been easy to live with, but her love for me has shone through.

I want to thank you, Nancy, for a wonderful marriage, and I pray we will be together forever.

13 January 2005

Jerry and Bonnie Moore: Our Friends

God gives us friends here on this earth
    To help us day by day
To help us and encourage us
    To help guide us on our way

Through thick and thin, good times and bad
    A true friend sticks close by
To share and bring some happy times
    And to hold you when you cry

God gives us all some special friends
    I know this is for sure
For God has blessed us with special friends
    In Jerry and Bonnie Moore

Pastor Jerry M. Moore, March 12, 1960 –
March 2, 2022

Testimony

On April 24, 2018, I returned home from a six-hour journey to Bainbridge, IN and back. After I got home, my wife decided to go shopping, and I took a bath. While in the tub, my chest started bothering me and my hands went numb. I did not think much about it and got out of the tub, made some phone calls, and did some work on my computer.

After about 20 minutes, my chest felt like it had kidney stones, so I texted my wife and told her I was going to the ER. I hopped in my truck and drove the seven miles to the hospital, while still having chest pains.

Within 10 minutes of laying down in the examination room, I died. They brought me back, then I died again. By that time, I had half of the emergency room staff in the room with me. I heard someone say they were going to send me to the Heart Center about fifty miles away.

By this time, someone from the ER contacted my wife via my cell phone and told her what was going on. I did get to see her shortly before they took me away.

They stuck me in an ambulance and rushed me to the Heart Center. As soon as I got there, I had to sign some paperwork, then was rushed into the operating room. Shortly after that, I died again. I remember when they brought me back this time, I looked up and saw all these faces looking at me. I said, "Where am I?"

They immediately started working on me. I was awake the whole time from the time I entered the ER to the time I got to my room after surgery. I was upchucking and dry heaving a lot and they did not want my airway to be compromised.

The whole time I was going through all of this, I was praying and singing hymns (inside my head). There was nothing else I could do, so I leaned on my faith and God blessed me throughout this ordeal. I do not ever remember being frightened of dying, or nervous about what was going on around and to me. God was definitely with me.

Every nurse and doctor who worked on me knew I was a Christian by my attitude and talk. In fact, the final report stated, "He is a very pleasant 63-year-old gentleman." I even discussed my faith with one of the hospital's maintenance workers when she visited my room.

I was very thankful for all of my visitors, my pastor, who I scared to death with this incident, friends from the Christian Motorcyclist's Association and people I have not seen for a while, and our son's pastor. Every one of them prayed with my wife and I and gave us the assurance that we were loved and prayed for.

My lovely wife, Nancy, was by my side the whole time, sleeping on a sofa in my room. It is such a joy to be married to this lovely lady.

I was treated wonderfully at the hospital, despite me giving everyone a hard time, but I know they enjoyed my wife and me. I can say beyond a shadow of a doubt that God was with my wife, family and I every step of the way. I know that I was in a lot of people's prayers, virtually worldwide. I felt the peace of God throughout this whole ordeal!

Thank You, Father, for the love that surrounded my family and I throughout this ordeal. Thank You for all of those who visited me, prayed for us and were there for us. Thank You for Your peace and grace that surrounded me, and still surrounds me as I slowly heal. It is wonderful to be a part of Your family. I do not know how people do it without You. I love You. Amen.

Scripture References

Old Testament

New Testament

Matthew
  5:14-16, Make Me a Beacon (62)
  6:19-20, You Can't Buy Your Way to
    Heaven (121)
  12:35, Another School Shooting (94)
  28:18-20, Preach It (43)

Mark
  16:15, I am a Christian (1)
  10:14-15, Joshua's Prayer (58)
  12:30-31, Love Your Neighbor (108)

Luke
  6:37, I am a Christian (2)

John
  1:14, Christmas Day is Over (100)
  3:16, I am a Christian (1)
  4:35, Fill Our Pews (16)

Romans
  3:23, I am a Christian (2), Salvation
    Through Christ (110)
  6:23, Salvation Through Christ (110)
  7:25, Every Second (31)
  8:28-29, Dear Father, Above (35)
  8:31, I am a Christian (2)
  8:38-39, Satan is Defeated (26)
  10:9-10, Salvation Through Christ (110)
  15:13, Instantaneously (29)

I Corinthians
> 2:9, When I Finally Get to Heaven (54)
> 15:52, In the Twinkling of an Eye (136)

II Corinthians
> 4:7-10, Do Not Despair (6)
> 4:17-18, There is Hope in You (42)
> 5:1-2, My Body (79)
> 5:10, My Reward (81)

Ephesians
> 4:13-15, God's Church Unite (46)
> 5:20, Praise Him (33)

Philippians
> 3:20-21, Just Another Day Closer (73)
> 4:1, I am a Christian (1)
> 4:13, Through Christ (69)

Colossians
> 3:1-4, One Day (7)
> 3:17, I Thank You (5)

I Thessalonians
> 5:16-18, Lord, Thank You (40)
> 5:18, God, Thank You (51)

I Timothy
> 2:1-3, Oh, Father God, We Need You (90)

II Timothy
> 4:2, Preach the Gospel (47)
> 4:18, My Final Ride (83)

Hebrews
> 4:16, Throne of Grace (8)

About the Author

 Kevin M. Pitzer likes to say he has three priorities in his life. Number one is God, number two is family and friends, and number three is his country. He was saved in a small church in New Castle, PA. He carried his faith throughout 34 years of military service and 29 years in Civil Service. He married Nancy in 1980 and has three children and seven grandchildren.

He retired in 2009 and enjoys puttering around his house and riding his Honda Goldwing Trike. He has been a member of The Christian Motorcyclist's Association since 2010. He has a Bachelor's Degree from Indiana Wesleyan University and a Master's Degree in Theological Studies from Liberty University Online.

He and his lovely wife live in Galveston, IN.

Please Visit and Like
"God and I"
On Facebook!